Knitting Patterns For Complete Beginners

Zackaryx .E Farleyg

Key advantages of learning to knit for mental health and wellbeing

Why is knitting so therapeutic and good for your body and brain?

Have you ever heard the expression, "Knit your way to happiness"? It is believed that knitting every day promotes happiness and calmness.

One of the most calming and unwinding activities you can engage in is knitting, which is also said to help with anxiety and reduce stress. Knitting improves memory, keeps you focused, and stimulates the brain. Knitting with others lessened loneliness and isolation. By keeping your hands occupied with knitting, you can break bad habits like reaching for unhealthy temptations like chips, cigarettes, or your phone. The last significant mental health benefit of knitting is making gifts for loved ones and volunteering in the community because it promotes wellbeing and positive feelings.

Here are five major health advantages of knitting and crocheting, along with reasons why you should start doing it to improve your mental and physical health.

KNITTING ELIMINATES STRESS AND ANXIETY

One of knitting's biggest health advantages is this.

Stress, anxiety, and depression can be managed with the help of knitting's calming effects. Because knitting requires concentration, which can be distracting, and because the texture and color of the yarn affect mood, knitting has been shown to help calm and still the mind. Distracting from mental symptoms can be made easier by the rhythmic movements and sense of focus. When you knit, your hands have something to do and your mind can easily wander to peaceful places.

It is healthy to be able to "switch off" the mind for a brief period of time each day. Both the body and the brain are calmed by the gentle movements of the yarn between the knitting needles. People often enter a state of mindfulness while knitting without even realizing it. The act of knitting while seated still lowers blood pressure and lowers heart rate.

Knitting improves memory and concentration.

Does knitting aid in concentration and memory enhancement? Knitting helps to use the brain because it demands concentration, memory, and processing speed. Knitting stimulates and keeps the brain healthy, according to scientific research. Knitting can involve a lot of counting, multiplying, and measuring, which makes your brain actively use its memory.

Knitting boosts self-confidence and social skills.

Knitting with others, both in person and online, fosters social connection, lessens loneliness and isolation, and as a result, has a positive impact on mental health. You could, for instance, combine going out with knitting. It is incredibly simple to take your knitting project with you, show off your progress, and gain inspiration from the work of others. With knitting, you can even meet new people because you share a common hobby, and holding knitting needles in your hands can help you get over shyness. You should be proud of yourself if you have mastered knitting techniques, followed a pattern or set of instructions, finished a knitting project, and created something.

Knitting can help you break bad habits and keep busy.

You will be less likely to reach for chips, cigarettes, your phone, or a glass of wine if you have knitting in your hands and keep your fingers busy knitting or crocheting. Knitting can help you break bad habits. It's also a great way to keep yourself occupied when you want some alone time. It's nice to have an activity you can engage in when you want some alone time because not everyone is very social. While knitting, you can also use the time to listen to audiobooks and let your imagination transport you to the fantastic worlds the authors have created.

ONE WAY TO GIVE BACK IS TO KNIT

Knitting for others, whether as a gift for close friends and family or to give back to their community, gives a sense of well-being and makes you feel good to give. This is a further benefit of knitting for mental health. You can be kind by volunteering your time and talents to make something for a loved one, teach someone how to make something, or create things for a good cause. Here are some suggestions for presents you can knit for others.

Contents

Knitting Getting Started 1
Basic Knitting Techniques And Instructions 13
    Making A Slipknot 13
    Casting On 15
Simple Knitting Stitches For Beginners 36
    1. Garter Stitch 36
    2. Stocking Stitch 41
    3. Ribbing 42
    4. Seed Stitch 46
    5. Moss Stitch 47
Simple Knitting Projects For Beginners 50
    1. Easy Knitted Leg Warmers 50
    2. DIY Finger Knit Rope Trivet 61
    3. Rib Ridge Dishcloth 69
Gift Ideas 71
    4. Toddler Slippers 71
    5. Easy Knit Mittens 77
    6. Child's Cat Hat 86
    7. DIY Knit Basket 88
    8. Heart Face Scrubby 89
    9. Knitted Floor Pouf 92
    10. Hand-knit Straight Tie 93
Scarves 96
    11. Garter Stitch Scarf 96
    12. Ionos Infinity Scarf 98

| 13. | One Row Handspun Scarf | 100 |

Blankets And Throws 102

14.	Simple Blanket	102
15.	Sunny Baby Blanket	109
16.	Double Seed Stitch Blanket	111

Shawls 113

17.	Quick and Easy Shawl	113
18.	Easy Lace Shawl	115
19.	Xcellent Shawl	117

Headbands 120

20.	Cable Headbands	120
21.	Newbie Knitted Headband	124
22.	Seed Stitch Headband	127

Cowls 132

23.	Ribbed Velvet Knit Cowl	132
24.	Seed Stitch Cowl	136
25.	Beginner Knit Cowl	139

Seasonal Projects 141

Summer 141
| 27. | Chunky Knit Boot Cuffs | 150 |

Winter 156
| 30. | Easy Arm Warmers | 159 |
| 31. | Garter Wrist Warmers | 162 |

Spring 164
| 33. | Simple Garter Stitch Knit Cowl | 167 |
| 34. | Color Blocked Afghan | 170 |

Autumn 174
| 36. | Knitted Pumpkin Pattern | 177 |
| 37. | Maple Leaf | 180 |

Dish Clothes 185

39.	Diamond Brocade	187
40.	Crazy Eights Dishcloth	189
Conclusion		191

Knitting Getting Started

The book uses an apprenticeship-like approach by focusing on the most important parts and avoiding anything that you will really not find useful in actually making your first knitted pieces. That's why the first chapter will focus primarily on what you will need to get started.

What You Will Need

Yarn

Yarn is basically the material you will be using in your knitting projects. It is a textile comprised of interlocked fibers (known as plies) that are wound together to make thicker strands. The fibers can be derived from either animals (e.g., sheep's wool, angora, or mohair) or plants (e.g. silk, hemp, or cotton). The type of yarn you need for your project will depend on the number of plies used in the textile, which leads to the following weight categories:

- Lace (Approximately 1 ply) – This yarn is extremely light and is commonly used to make cute lace designs. You need to handle it delicately to avoid breakage or tangling.
- Super Fine, Fine, and Light (Approximately 2-5 ply) – This weight category will provide great stitch definition in your hats, scarves, sweaters, and mittens.
- Bulky and Super Bulky (Approximately 12-14 ply) – Use this yarn when you need to work on a big project (such as a blanket, throw, chunky scarf, etc.) quickly and efficiently. For optimal loft, knit using loose, large stitches.

Knitting Needles

Knitting needles can be grouped into five main categories:

1. Straight needles

These are the most common types of needles and are probably what comes to mind when you think about knitting needles. Straight needles come in pairs, with each needle featuring a stopper or knob at one end and a point at the other. They are simple and easy to use and are the most recommended for beginners.

Most straight needles are 9-14 inches long, but there are shorter and longer ones in the market too. They are usually made with steel, aluminum, wood, bamboo, and even plastic. You will find that some types of yarn stitch better with needles created with certain materials, so feel free to experiment with different types if you feel that your yarn is not sliding smoothly along the needles. Straight needles are suitable for small projects that do not require a lot of dexterity, such as scarves or wash clothes.

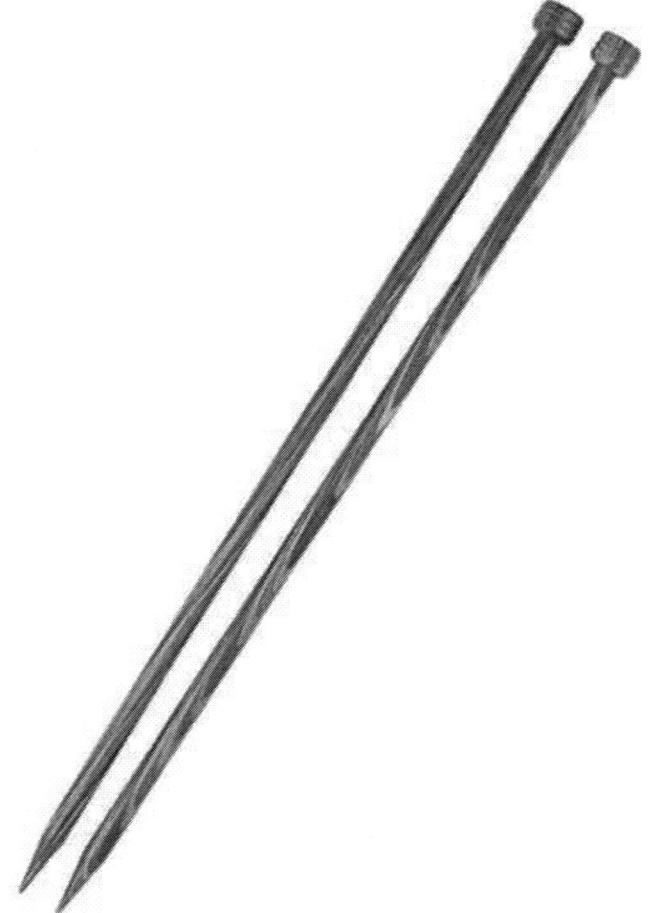

2. Circular needles

These needles are designed for large projects that you knit in the round. They are usually joined by a flexible cord that makes them look like one long needle, although there are fixed circular needles that are permanently connected at the cord and the ends.

Circular needles are typically 16-48 inches long, but, like with straight needles, you can find shorter or longer ones in the market. Similarly, wood, bamboo, plastic, aluminum, and steel are the most commonly used materials. For the cord, manufacturers normally use coated steel or nylon.

Note that some circular needles have a memory or tend to hold their shape, which can make them difficult to control. As such, be sure to look for "memory-free" needles when shopping for your tools. Use circular needles for items that are knitted in the round, for example, socks, cowls, hats, and sweaters.

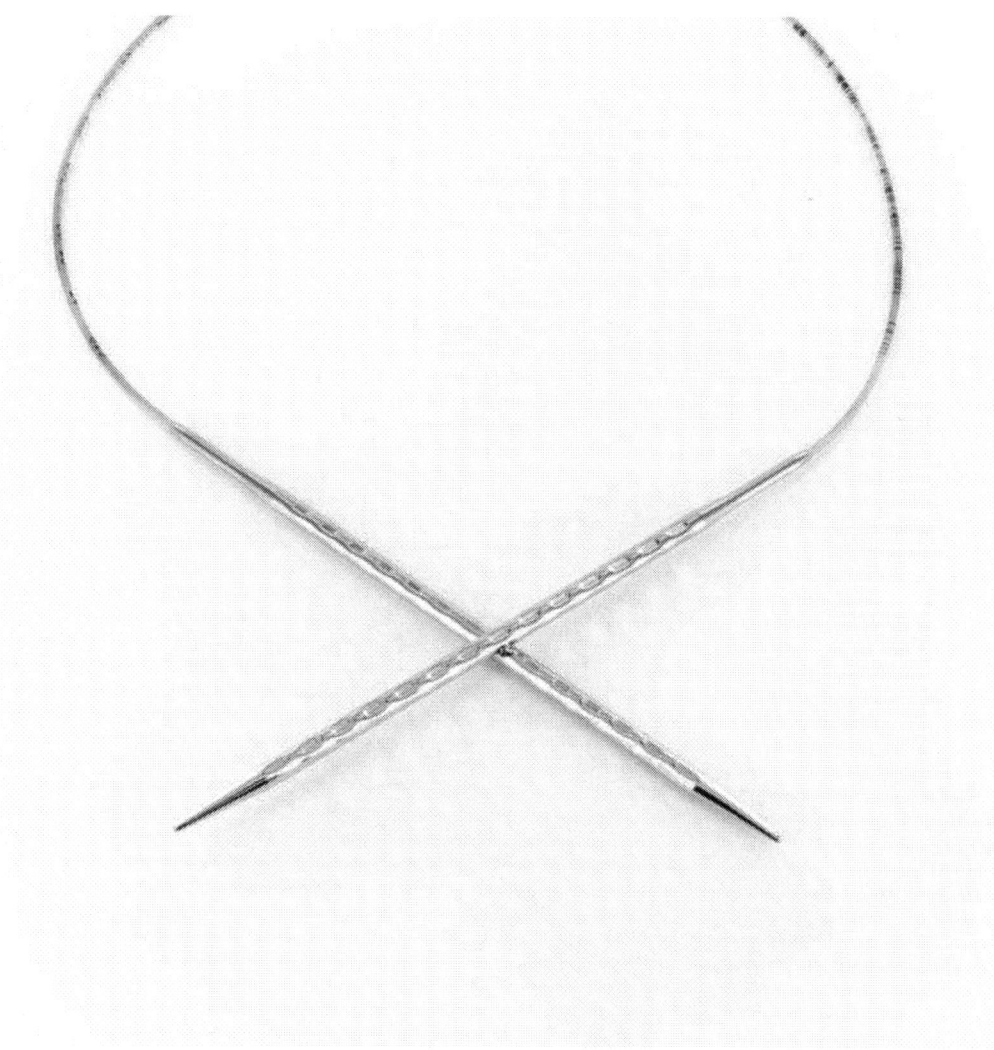

3. Interchangeable needles

These needles solve the issue of versatility that is limited in circular needles, all while offering the same flexibility in different sizes. They come with a flexible cord and a firm tip, just like their cousins, the circular needles, but you can adjust the cord lengths and needle sizes by separating the pieces. You can also use them as straight needles by connecting the needles to the cords, then attaching caps at the ends. Interchangeable needles are sold both as individual pieces as well as in sets.

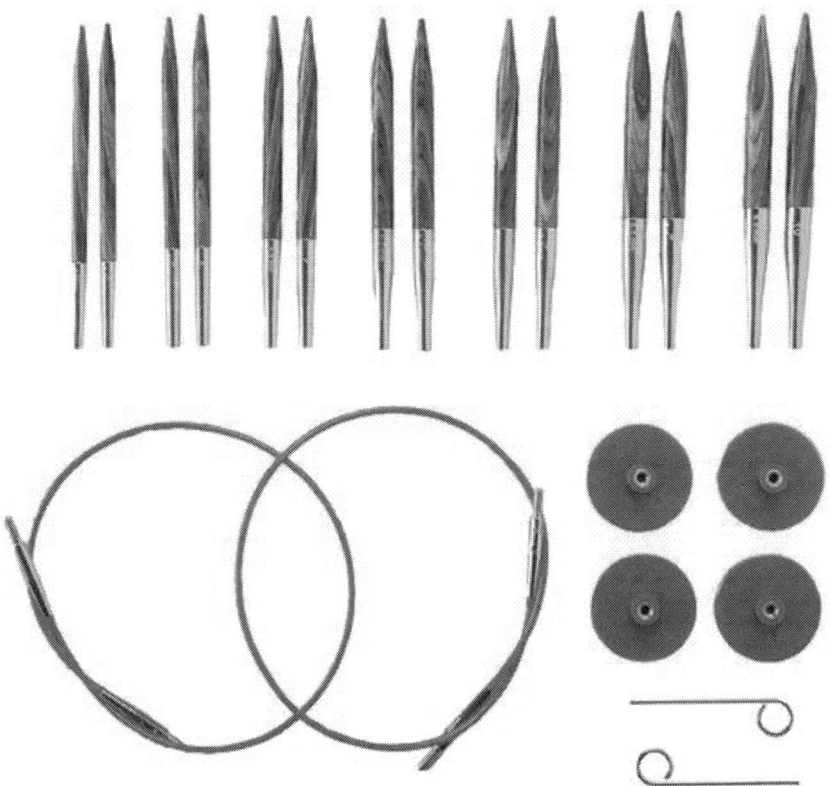

4. Double-pointed needles

These needles are also great for knitting small items in the round, but they are more like the shorter versions of straight needles with points at both ends. Some DPNs come with either a flexible portion or a bend in the middle. Unlike the regular DPNs that are sold in sets of 4-6 needles, these ones are packed in sets of 3 because the flexible portion allows you to stitch with fewer needles. DPNs are usually 5-8 inches long, but there are longer needles designed for knitting tubular-shaped items such as hats and shorter ones for tiny projects like children's socks.

5. Cable needles

Designed for holding stitches when creating knitted cables, these needles have an odd, double-pointed shape and are used to protect active stitches while knitting in the round. As they are only meant to hold a few stitches temporarily, these types of needles are just a couple of inches in length. You have a number of options to choose from in terms of material, including glass, wood, bamboo, plastic, and metal.

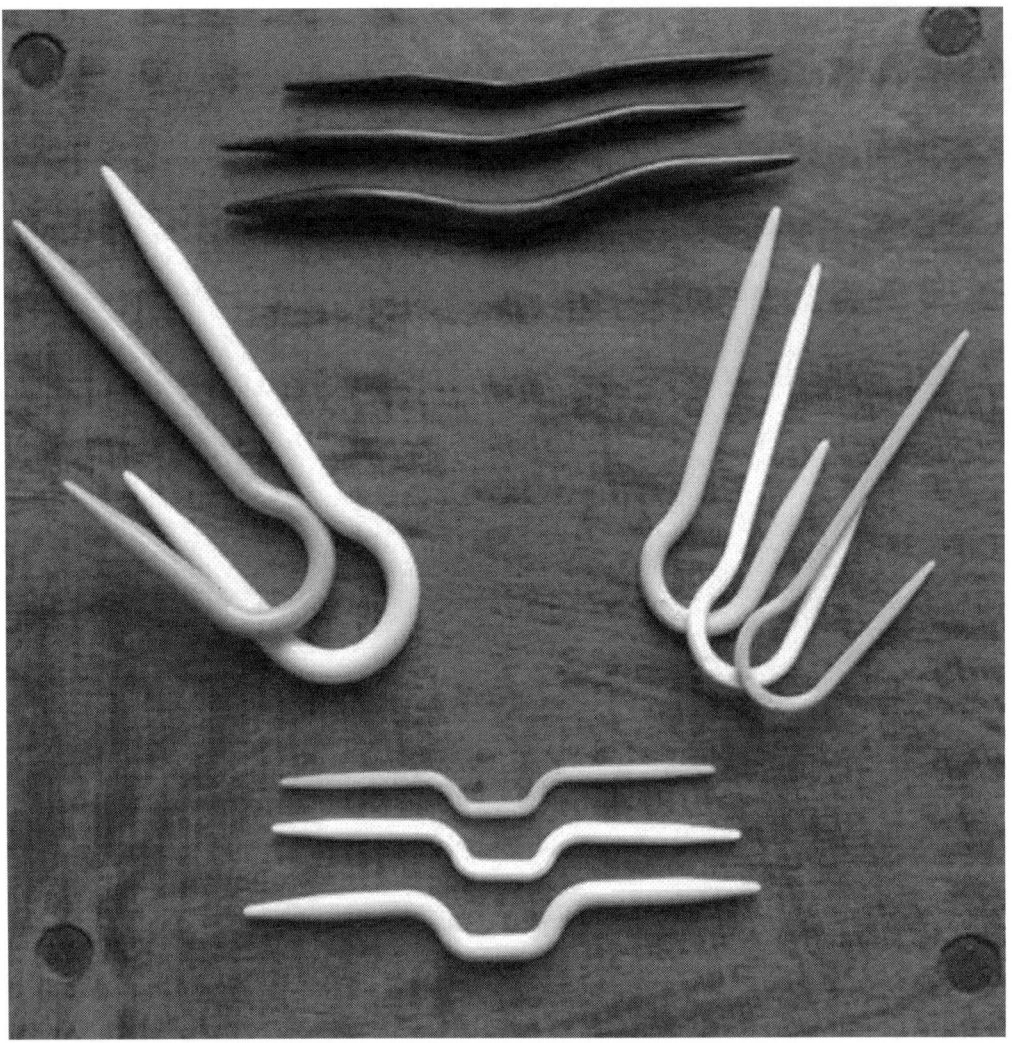

Others

Apart from yarn and knitting needles, you need to get a few other tools before you start your knitting project. These include:

1. Scissors – to cut off the extra yarn
2. Sewing needles – to weave in the ends and to sew together two or more pieces of an item such as the arms of a sweater. Be sure to look

for "tapestry needles" or "yarn needles" that have large enough eyes for your yarn to fit through.

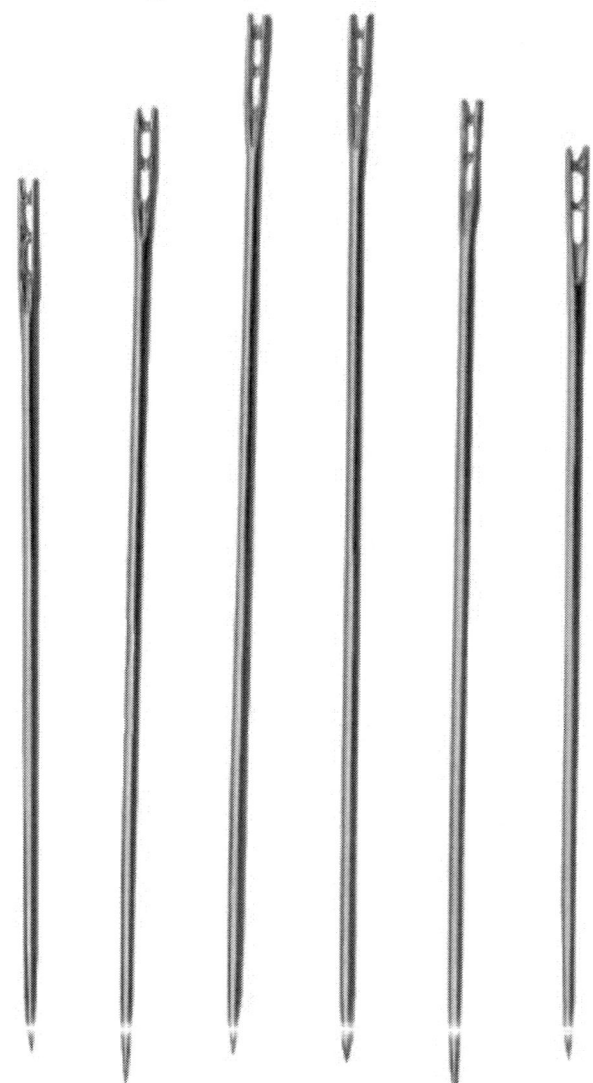

3. Crochet hooks – if you are unable to weave in the ends of your yarn because they are too short, you'll be glad to have a crochet hook in your tool box. Sizes G and H are great for most weight categories of yarn, and they are easy to use even if you have never crocheted in

your whole life.

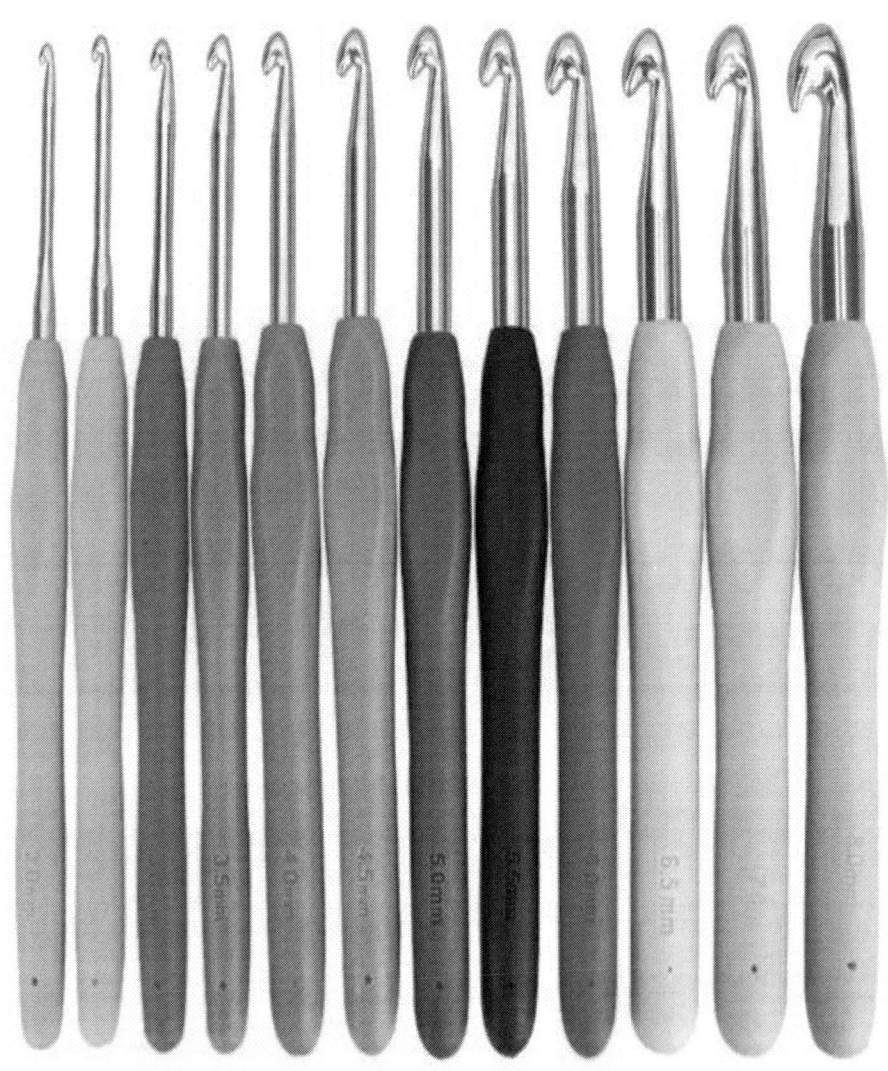

Once you have acquired these tools, you are ready to begin your first project. But before we sail off, let's get acquainted with a few

preliminaries.

Basic Abbreviations

Once you have familiarized yourself with the knitting basics, you will be ready to begin your first knitting project. When surfing through knitting patterns for the first time, it can feel like you've just crept into some sort of knitting Narnia, where things are explained in a special language consisting of codes and terms with hidden meanings. This is because the world of knitting is characterized by many terms and abbreviations, but don't let this get into your head. These abbreviations are only used to save space and make it easier to read patterns. Most of the projects in this book that are abbreviated have the special abbreviations listed and explained, but the most common ones include:

- P = purl stitch

- K= knit stitch

- Work even = continue, without increasing or decreasing

- Tog = together = work at least two stitches together to form a decrease

- YO = yarn over = bring the yarn over your needle

- Sl = Slip = slide a stitch(es) from needle 1 to needle 2, without working it

- Rep = repeat = repeat what you were doing as many times as the pattern calls for

- Dec = decrease = remove a stitch(es). In many cases, this basically involves working two stitches into one, which is doable in both K and P

- Inc = increase = add a stitch(es). This usually involves working in the front of a stitch, then in the back, which is also doable in both K and P stitches.

Note that there are several ways to increase and decrease, all of which will affect the final outlook of your project. So be sure to use the one specified in the pattern if you are following the project to the letter.

- BO = bind off = Also known as casting off, this is the final step in knitting, and it simply means wrapping up your project so that it does not fall apart once you are done.

- CO = cast on = This marks the beginning of your knitting project. It basically means mounting your stitches and yarn onto your knitting needles.

Now that you know what you need and the abbreviations you are likely to encounter, we can move to the next part, which is knitting – creating stitches and more.

Basic Knitting Techniques And Instructions

Making A Slipknot

Most knitting projects begin with a slipknot. Follow these simple steps to learn how to make a slipknot.

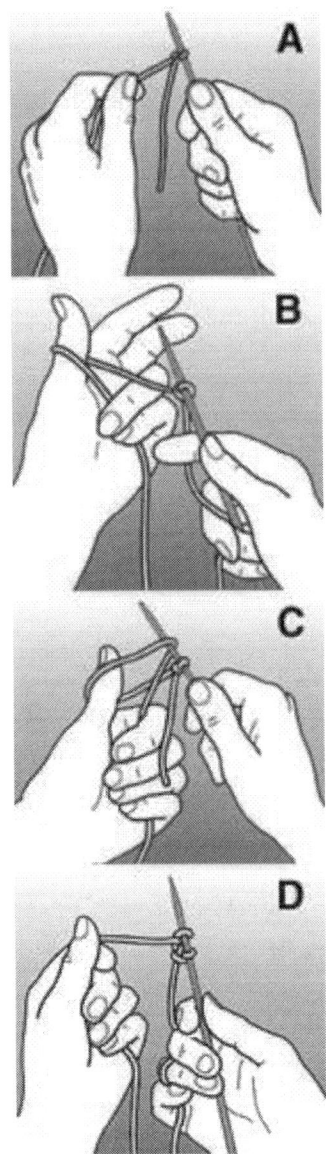

1. Start by placing the tail of your yarn in front of your palm, then, on your left hand, loosely loop the yarn around your first two fingers.

2. Pull the thread from the ball of yarn under the one behind your fingers, then pass it through the loose loop.

3. Grab the new loop with your right hand and the tail with your left hand, then tighten by pulling the tail to create your slipknot.

Casting On

Casting on simply means putting your stitches and yarn onto the needles and is usually the first step in making a knitting pattern.

There are several methods of casting on, starting from the most basic one:

A) Single cast on – this is the simplest way to cast on.

i) Start by forming a slipknot from the slipknot instructions.

ii) Slide the slipknot onto your needles and tighten the knot by pulling the yarn.

iii) Wrap the yarn attached to the ball around your thumb to create a loop.

iv) Pass your needle under, then up through this loop with your thumb still in place.

v) Remove your thumb, then pull the yarn.

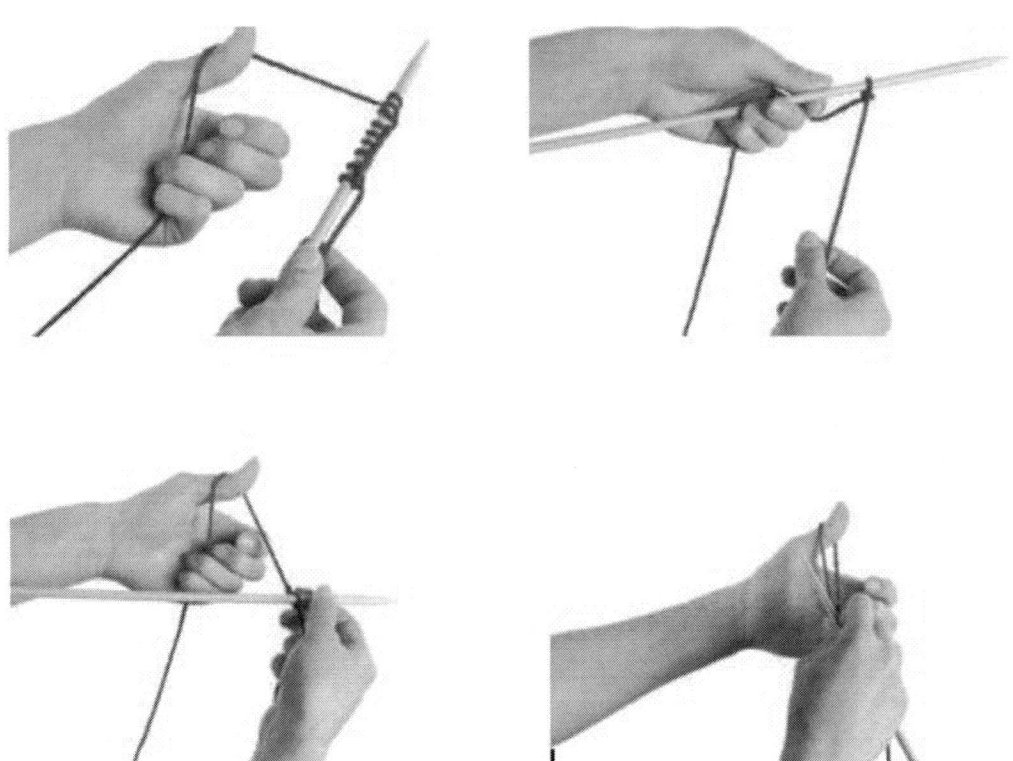

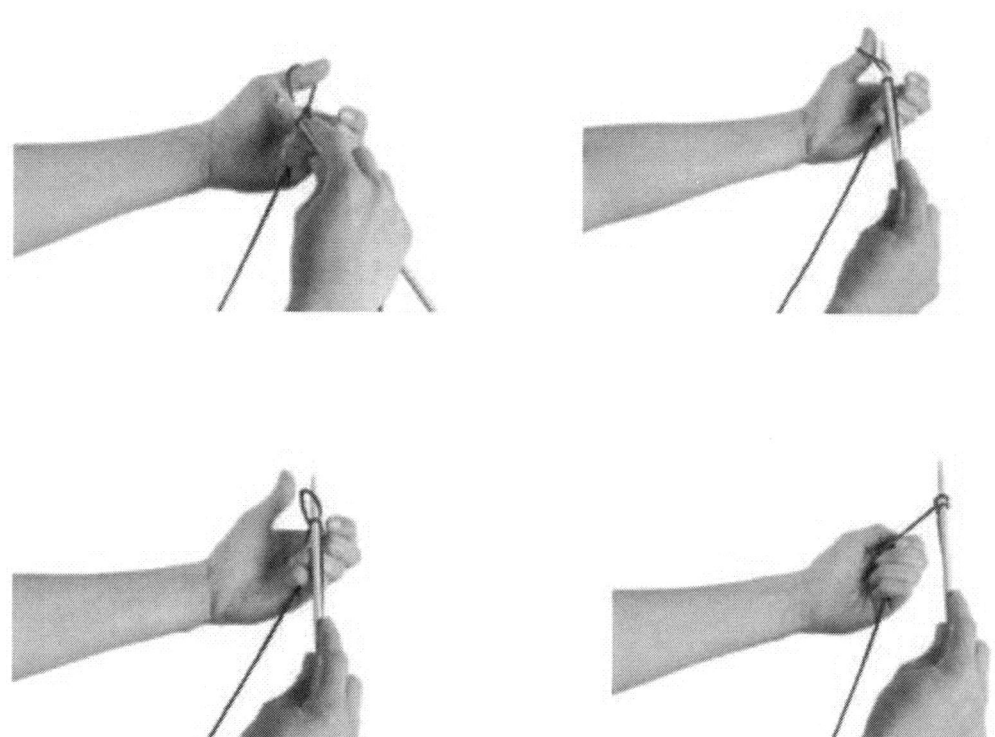

B) Long-tail cast on.

i) Start by leaving a tail of thread from your yarn, depending on how many stitches you are casting on. A foot of tail, for example, should be enough if you're casting on ten stitches.

ii) Put the tail loosely over the pointer finger and thumb of your left hand..

iii) Hold it in between the middle and pointer finger.

iv) Using your ring and pinky finger, hold the thread attached to the big yarn against your palm.

v) Using your right hand, place the needle over the yarn between your pointer finger and thumb.

vi) Form a loop around your thumb by pulling the needle (along with the yarn) towards you.

vii) Pass the needle below the yarn right beside your thumb, then up across the loop.

viii) Pull the needle towards the pointer finger again.

ix) Drape the needle over the yarn attached to the pointer finger, then pull it under towards your thumb again.

x) Bring the head of your needle down across the loop on your thumb.

xi) Remove your thumb, then pull the yarn.

xii) Start again from step 7 until you cast on the number of stitches you need.

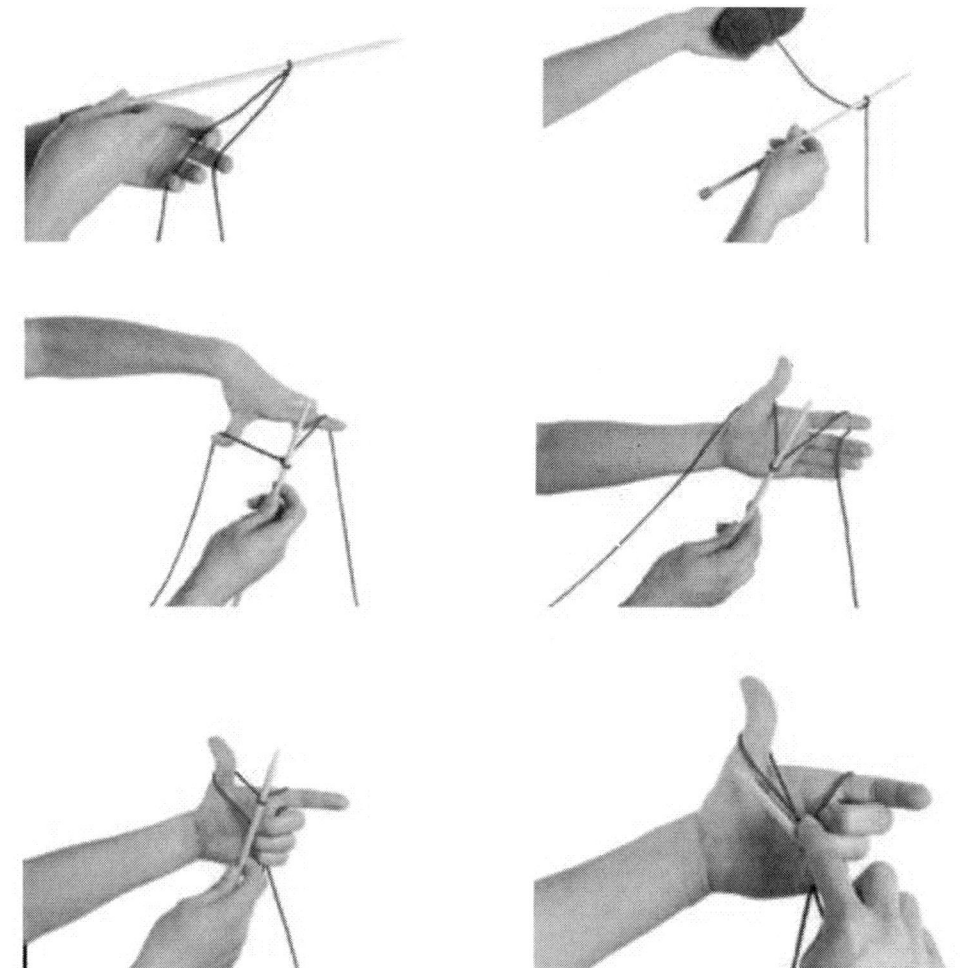

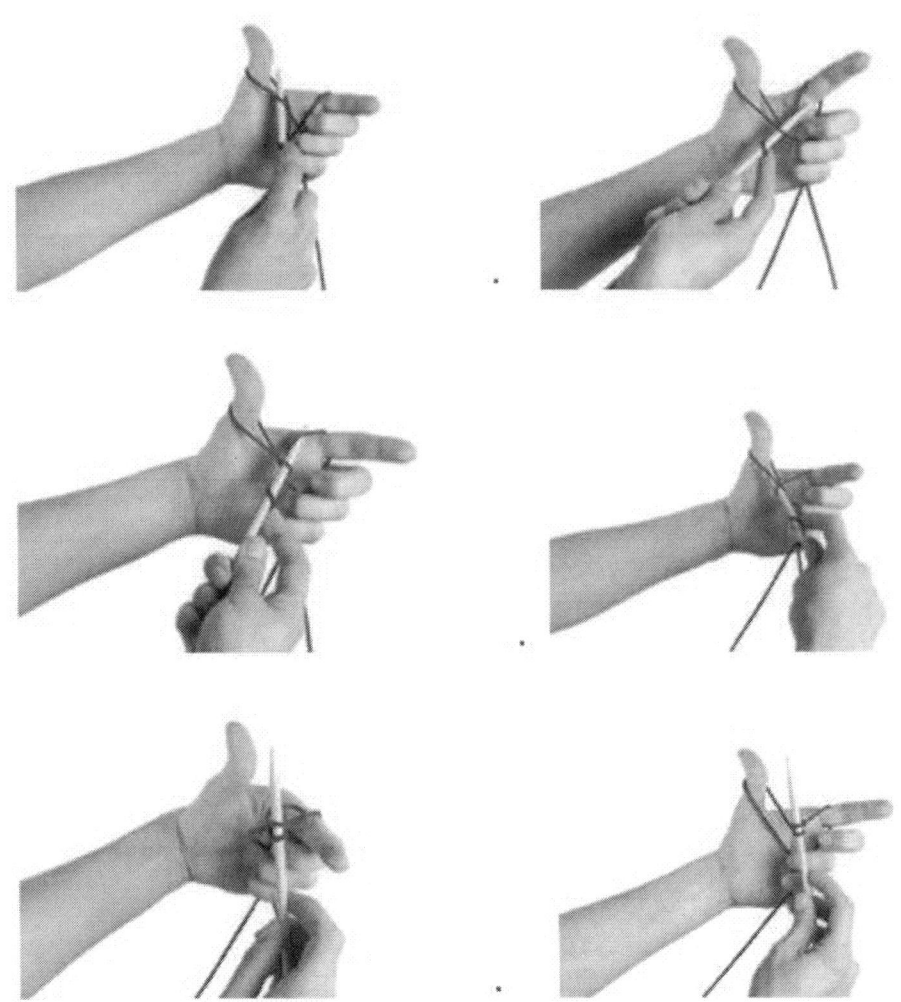

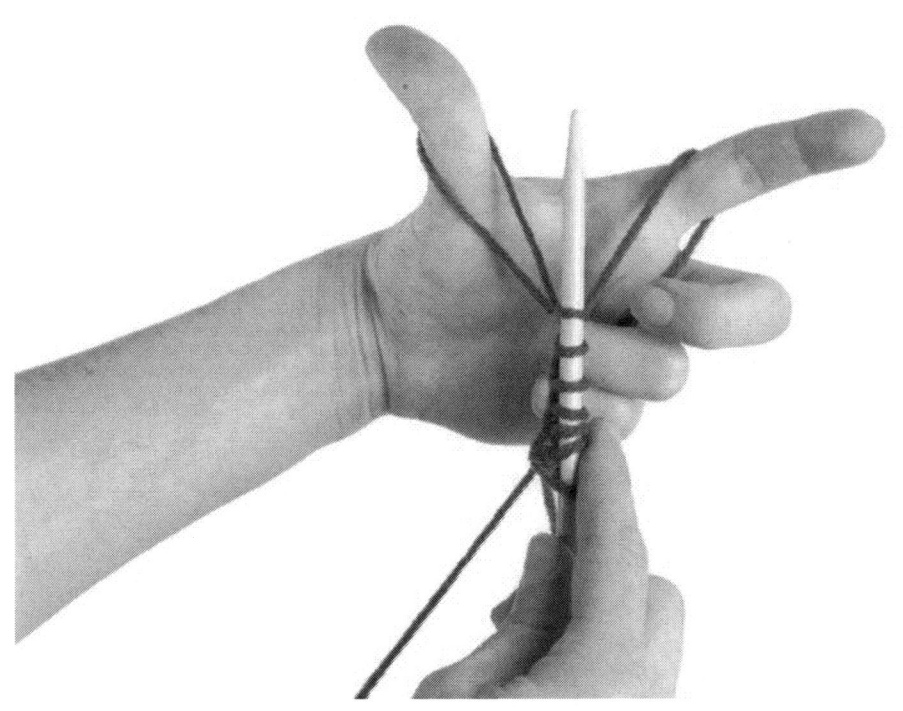

C) Knit Cast On

i) Start by creating a slipknot, then place it on your first needle on the left hand. Use your right hand to hold the second needle.

ii) Pass the second needle through the loop formed on the left hand when creating the slipknot.

iii) Wrap the yarn you are working with around the needle on your left hand, using your left hand.

iv) Bring the needle on your right hand through the left loop again, to create a new loop on the right side.

v) Turn and drop the new loop onto your left needle, then remove the needle on your right hand from the loop.

vi) Finish casting on your two stitches by pulling the yarn.

vii) Remove from the second step to continue.

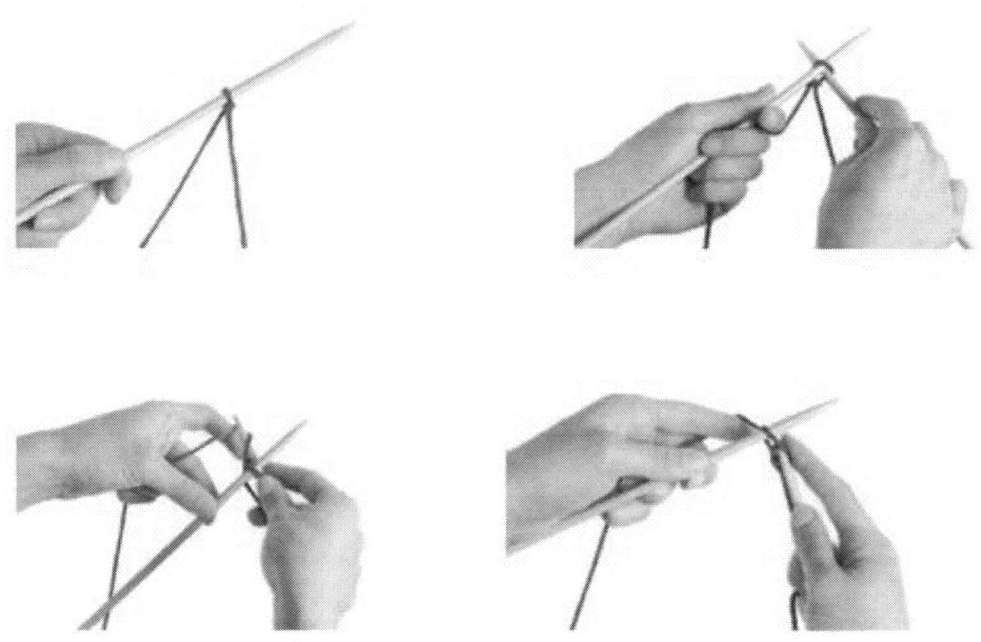

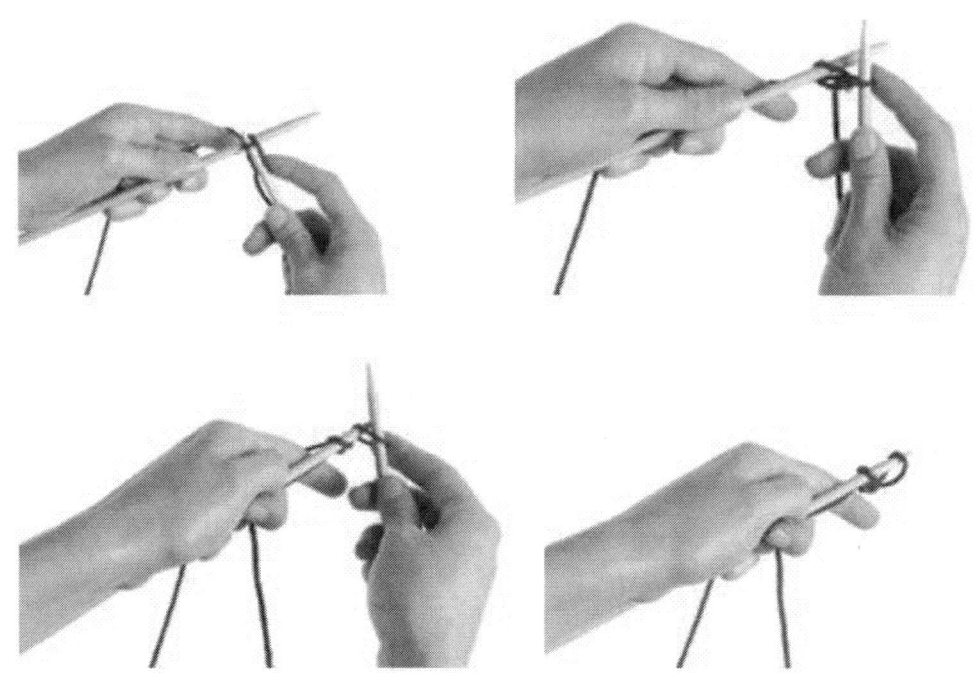

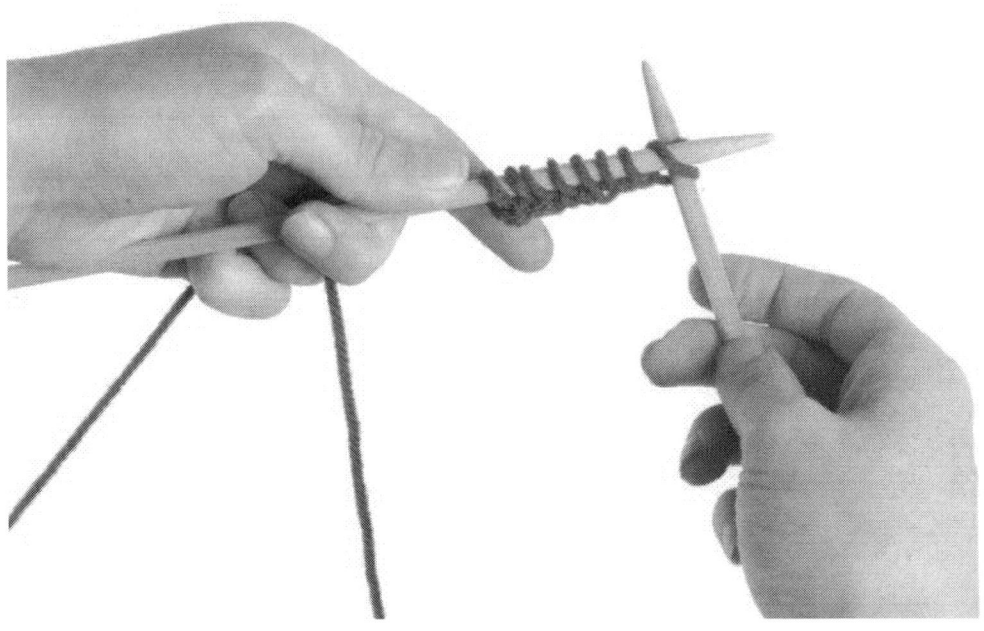

D) Cable cast-on

i) Use the "knit cast on" instructions to cast on the first 2 stitches.

ii) Bring the needle on your right hand under the one on your left, then put it through the yarn connecting the two stitches, so that it sits in between.

iii) Wrap the yarn you're working with around the needle on your right.

iv) Pull the right-hand needle through the loops again to form a new loop on your right hand.

v) Turn and drop this new loop onto the needle on your left, then release the right-side needle.

vi) Finish your cable cast on by pulling the yarn.

vii) Repeat from the second step to continue.

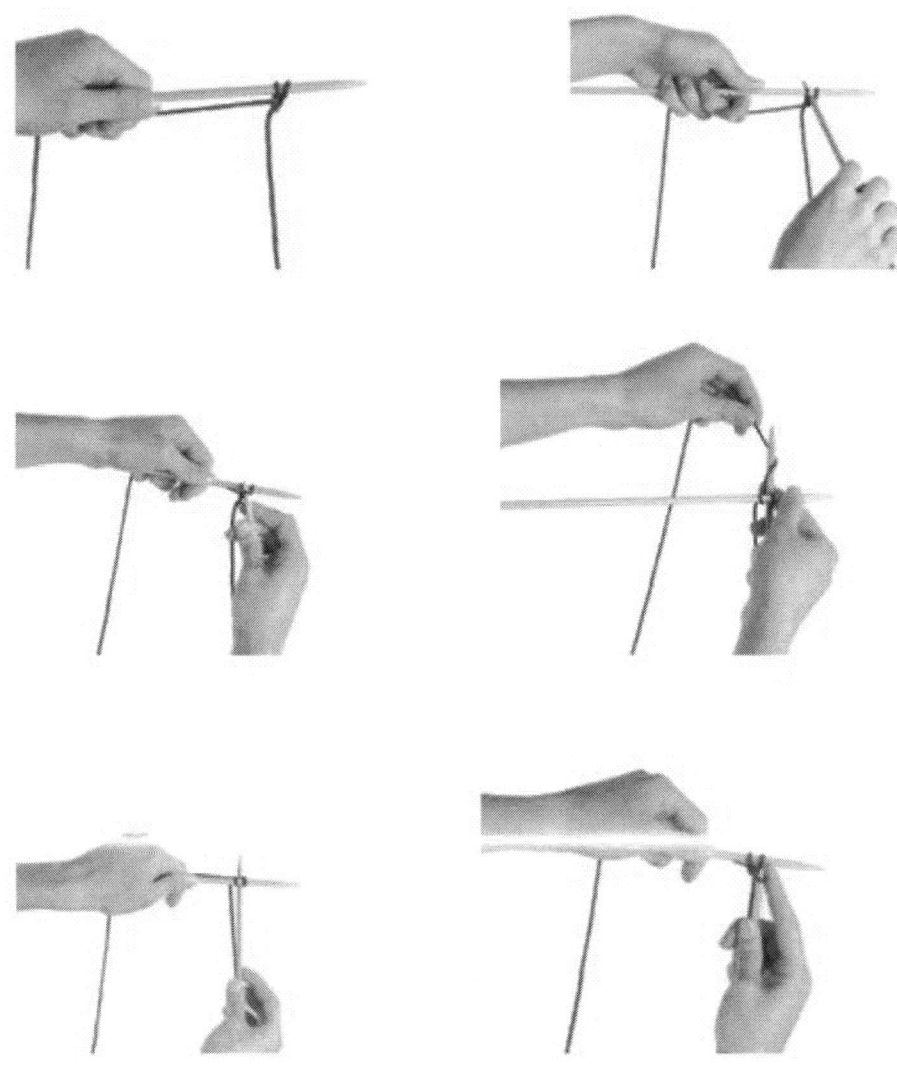

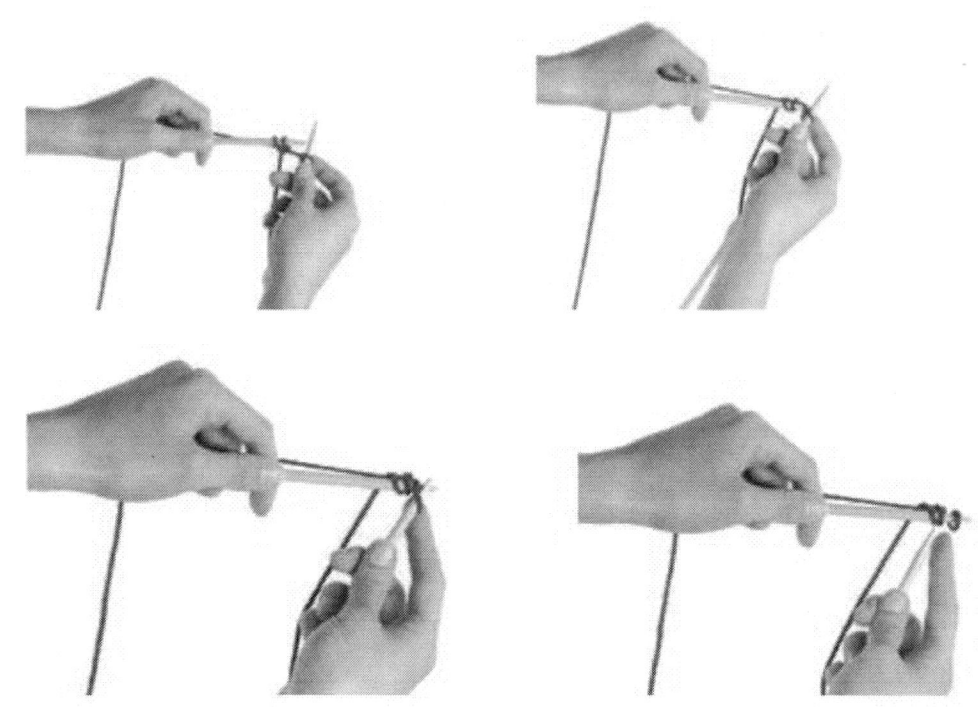

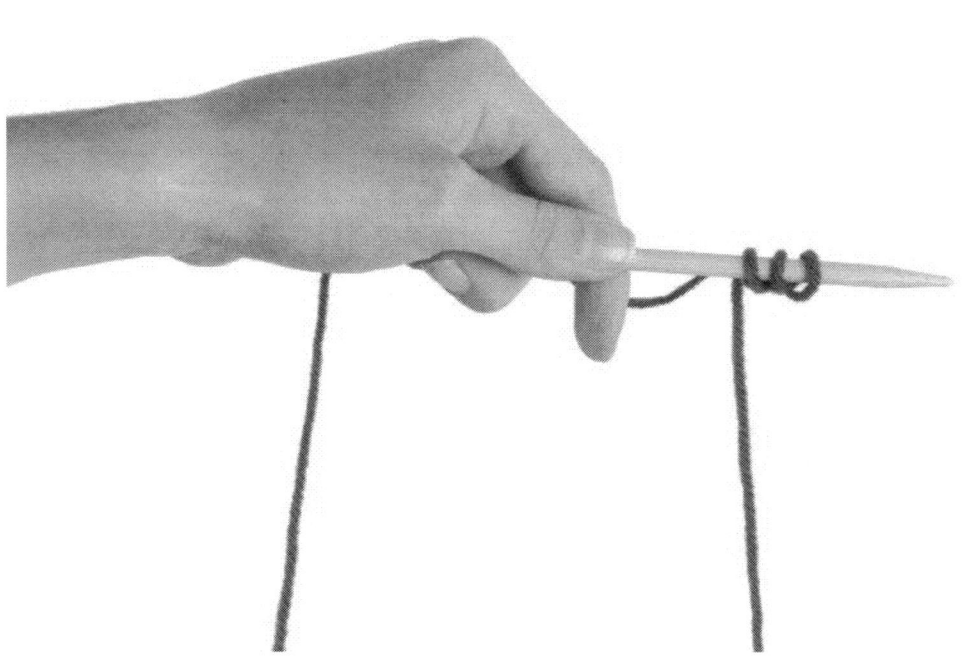

How To Cast Off/Bind Off

Once you are done knitting, you will need to do one last thing to keep your project from unraveling. This step is referred to as casting off or binding off. Below is a photo tutorial explaining how to bind off in 12 simple steps.

1) Loosely knit 2 stitches.

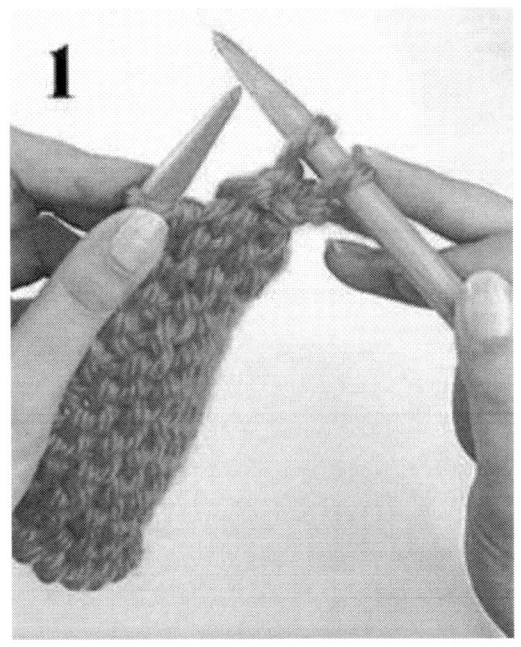

ii) Slide the needle on your left into the first stitch.

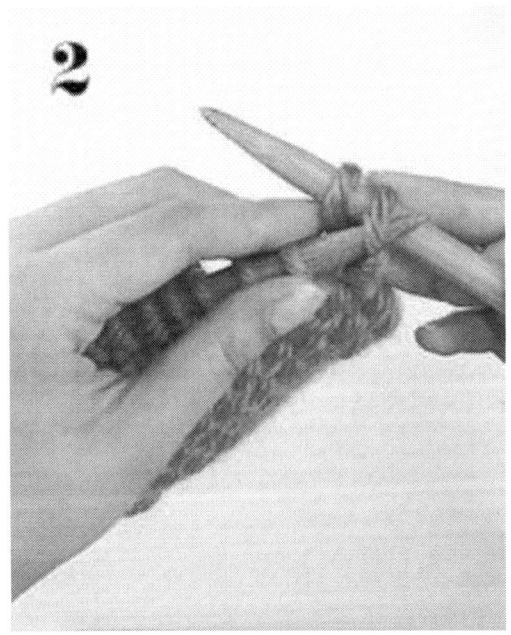

iii) Pull that stitch over stitch two.

iv) Continue pulling until the stitches are off the needle.

v) You have now cast off one stitch while the other is on the right side needle.

vi) Knit 1 stitch and repeat from step 2 to 6 until you are left with one stitch.

vii) With one stitch remaining, cut off a ten-inch tail of yarn.

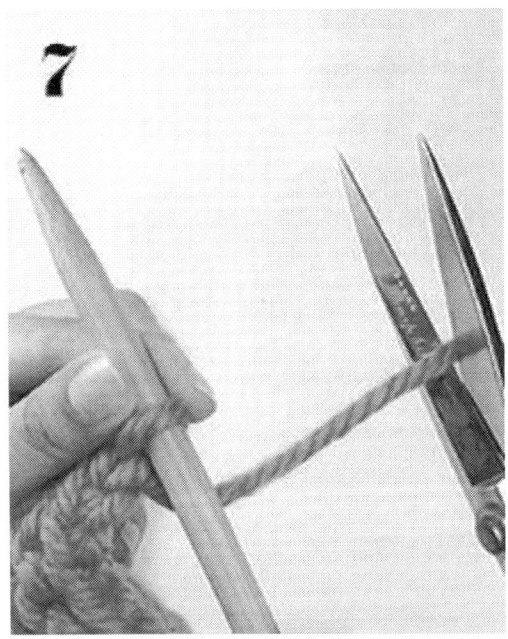

viii) Wrap the tail around your needle.

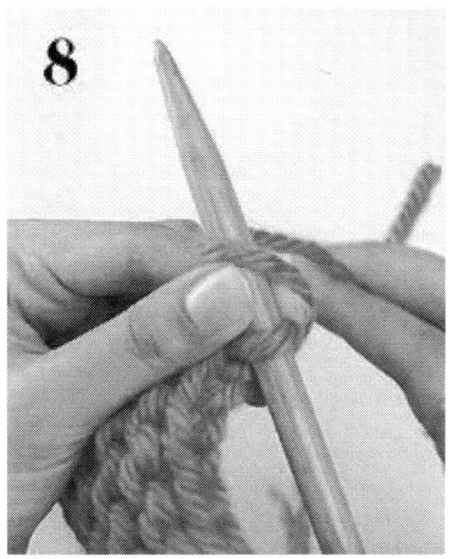

ix) Slide the remaining stitch over the tail.

x) Pass the tail across the needle.

xi) Tighten the tail by pulling.

xii) You have successfully cast off your knitting!

With what we've learned so far in mind, let's move to the knitting stitches you need to know.

Simple Knitting Stitches For Beginners

1. Garter Stitch

The garter stitch is one of the most popular (and one of the simplest) stitches in the knitting world. Knitters often use it when they are looking to achieve a stripped texture on their edges or borders, without curling. It is also perfect for creating thick, strong, and slightly flexible fabrics.

How to do the garter stitch

Tools and materials

- Yarn

- Knitting needles

Instructions

- Knit the first stitch. The garter stitch is typically made up of knit stitches. Therefore, you need to start by making your first knit stitch once you are done casting on. Next, insert the right-sided needle from the front to the back of your first stitch, left to right.

- Bring your yarn around the right-hand needle. Wrap it counterclockwise so that it comes between the right and left-hand needles.

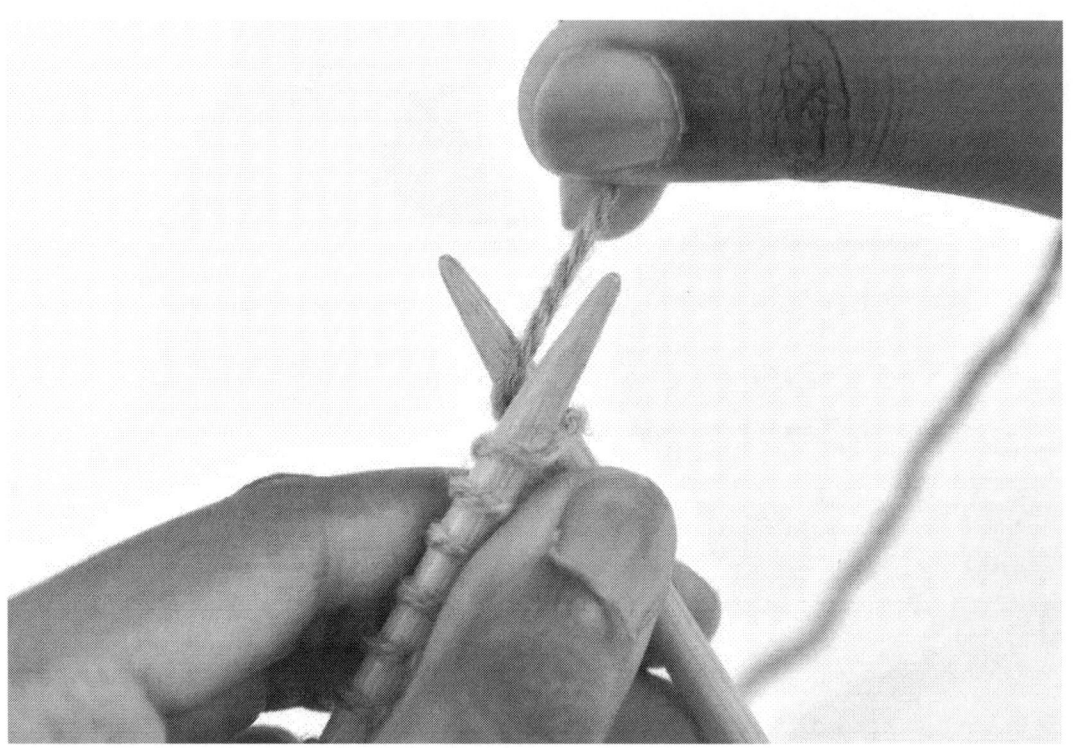

- Push the right-hand needle in front. Slide it under the left-hand needle and bring it (along with the working yarn) to the front to create a new stitch on your right-hand needle.

- Push the completed stitch from the left-hand needle onto the stitch on the right. This makes up your first knit stitch.

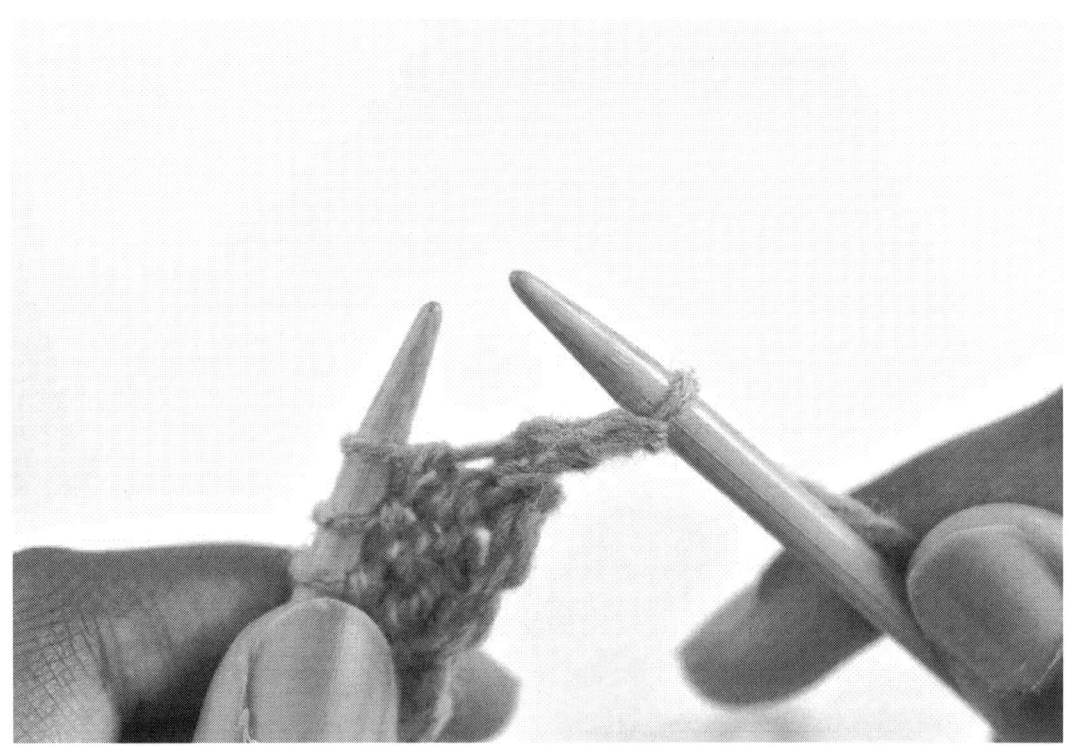

- Work all the knit stitches. All you have to do now is repeat the steps for making the first knit stitch until you achieve the number of stitches you need across the row.

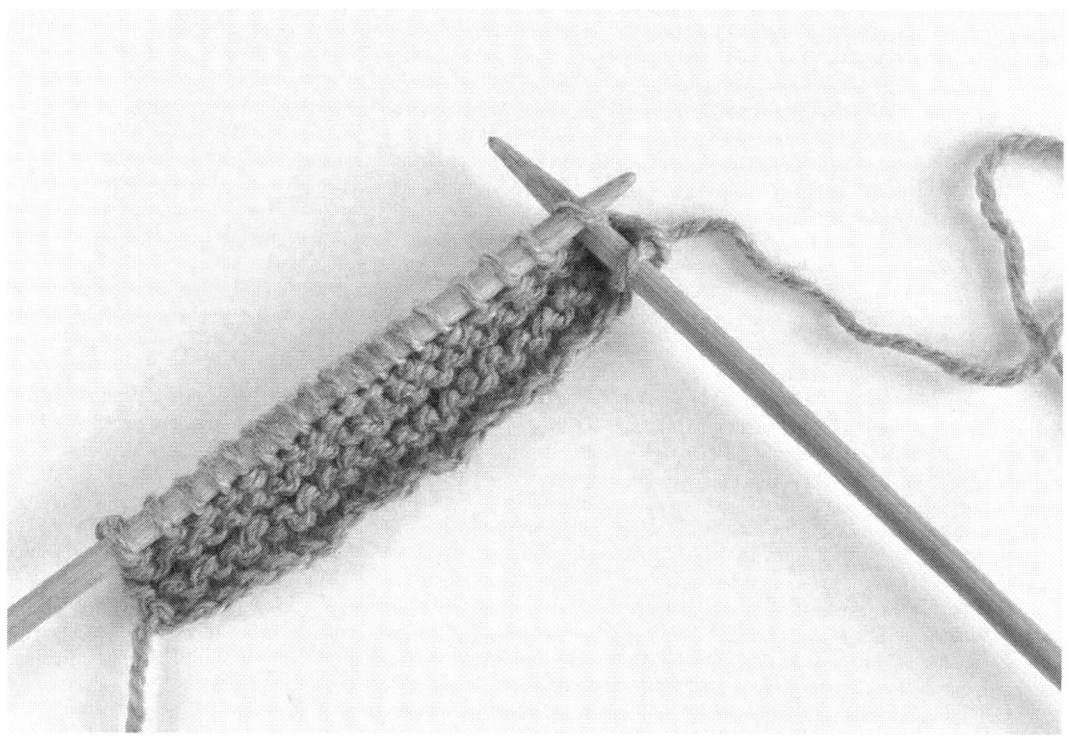

2. Stocking Stitch

The stocking (stockinette) stitch is another simple and popular knitting stitch that you can use without worrying about the number of stitches you are working with per row, whether it's an even or odd number. If you are knitting in the round, you can form the stockinette stitch by working all the stitches of every round (without purling, as the direction of knitting does not change when working in the round).

How to do the stocking stitch

- First row: knit across

- Second row: purl across

- Do these two rows repeatedly until you reach the desired length

This stitch produces what is commonly called "knit fabric," whose front is characterized by a series of V-like formations while the back looks like waved ridges.

An alternate version of the stocking stitch is the reverse stockinette stitch, which is made by purling the first row and knitting the second, so that the purled side appears in the front

3. Ribbing

Once you have experimented with knitting and purling in whole rows, you can begin alternating the two styles in the same row. Several possibilities immediately present themselves when you do this, but the most basic one is referred to as ribbing. Ribbing describes patterns in which you alternate knits and purls consistently along the rows until you end up with similar-looking columns across the fabric. You can use this method for your edges only or for the entire knitting project.

Ribbing is further subdivided into different forms, depending on the number of stitches of each type that should be worked in order. The most used ones are the "1X1" rib (where you knit 1 and purl 1, then repeat) and the "2X2" rib (where you knit 2 and purl 2, then repeat), but you can use virtually any combination in ribbing, whether it's 3X1 or 4X4. Just be sure to cast on the right number of stitches for the pattern you are following. For example, you need an even number of stitches to do the 1X1 rib, and a multiple of four stitches to do the 2X2 rib.

How to do the rib stitch (hat)

Tools and materials

- 100 yards of yarn (bulky weight)

- Yarn needle

- Scissors

- Ruler

- 10 (6mm) knitting needles

Instructions

- Start by casting on 72 stitches using the long-tail method

- 1st row: Knit2, Purl2, repeat up to 8 inches in length

Start decreasing the stitches to shape the upper part of your hat:

- 2nd row: K2, P2tog; repeat up to 54 stitches

Work even the next three rows using the stockinette stitch method

- 3rd row: P all the stitches

- 4th row: K all the stitches

- 5th row: P all the stitches

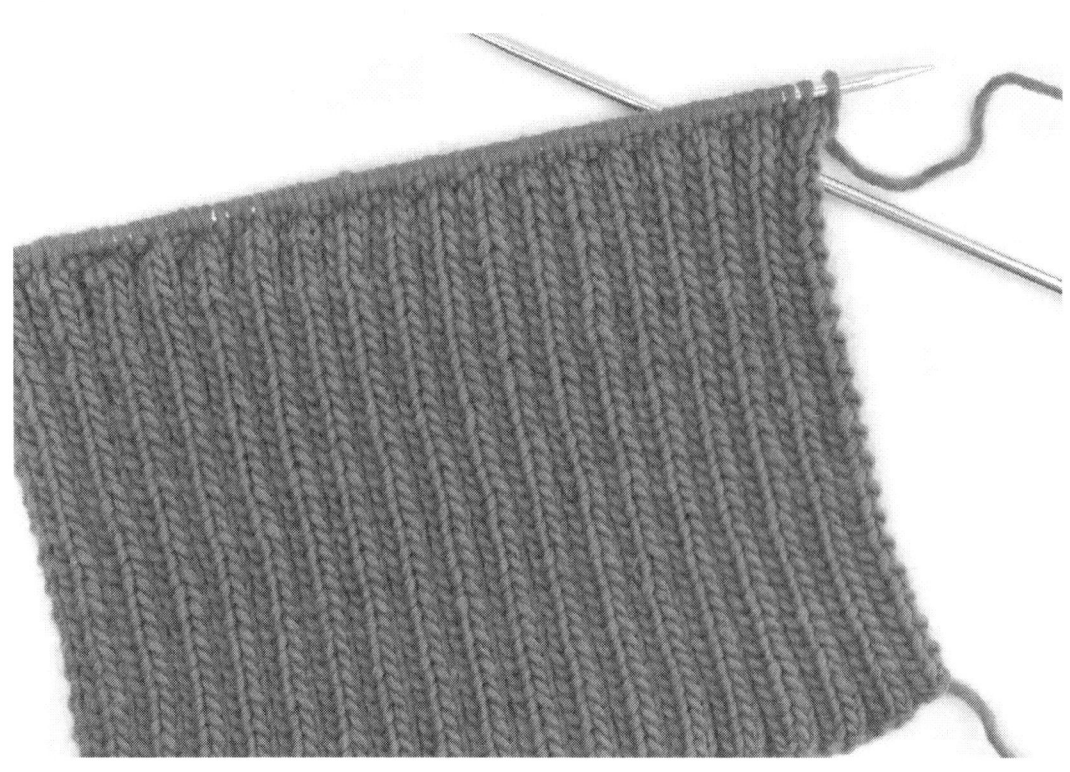

Completing hat shaping

- 6th row: K2tog; repeat up to 27 stitches

- Cast off using purl stitches, and set apart a long tail before cutting the yarn

Finishing

- Join both of the edges, with the seam centered behind the hat. Pass the yarn tail through the yarn needle and sew it into the folded edge. Weave together the upper part of the hat, as well as the back. Seam starting from up going down.

4. Seed Stitch

The seed stitch is quite similar to ribbing but, instead of consistently alternating your knits and purls in columns, you alternate them on each row. This leads to a pattern of individual knits and purls, which alternate both vertically and horizontally (that is, without stacking on each other). The technique got its name from the little bumps of purls that resemble seeds. It is excellent for knitting items that look similar on both sides, such as scarves, since both the front and back have the same appearance (the little bumps on one side are valleys on the other side, and vice versa).

How to do a seed stitch with even stitches

1ˢᵗ row: Knit1, Purl1, Repeat until the end of the row

2ⁿᵈ row: Purl1, Knit1, repeat to the end of the row

How to do a seed stitch with odd stitches

1ˢᵗ row: Knit1, Purl1, repeat to the last stitch, then finish with K1

Rows 2 to end: repeat what you did in row 1

5. Moss Stitch

The moss stitch is a slight variation of the seed stitch that is characterized by a pattern with a keen resemblance to tiny basket weaves. To do it, you simply alternate knits and purls after each stitch, then adjust their position every two rows.

There is no curling in the moss stitch, since the knits and purls are balanced. Like the seed stitch, this style is reversible, which makes it ideal for projects whose fabric is commonly seen on both sides, such as blankets and scarves.

However, it is important not to confuse between a moss stitch and seed stitch. The simplest way to differentiate between the two techniques is to remember that the seed stitch starts with a single row of K1, P1 repeats, while the moss stitch begins with two rows of the same repeats. Nevertheless, you can usually use the moss stitch for many projects that are based on the seed stitch. Just be sure to adjust the number of stitches if the original pattern started with an odd number (as the moss stitch is worked on multiples of 2 with a 4-row repeat).

How to moss stitch

1st row: Knit1, Purl1, repeat across

2nd row: Knit1, Purl1, repeat across

3rd row: Purl1, Knit1, repeat across

4th row: Purl1, Knit1, repeat across

Start again, repeating the 4 rows for the rest of the pattern

Now that you understand the stitches, we can now move to create simple patterns that use these stitches.

Simple Knitting Projects For Beginners

1. Easy Knitted Leg Warmers

Tools and materials

Two skeins (200g) of yarn

Size 11 knitting needles

Instructions

Cast on 5 stitches

Spread the stitches, then double each by knitting on their front and back. You will have to adjust the stitches on your needles once you finish working on the first 2 stitches. Use a different colored piece of yarn to mark where the first round begins.

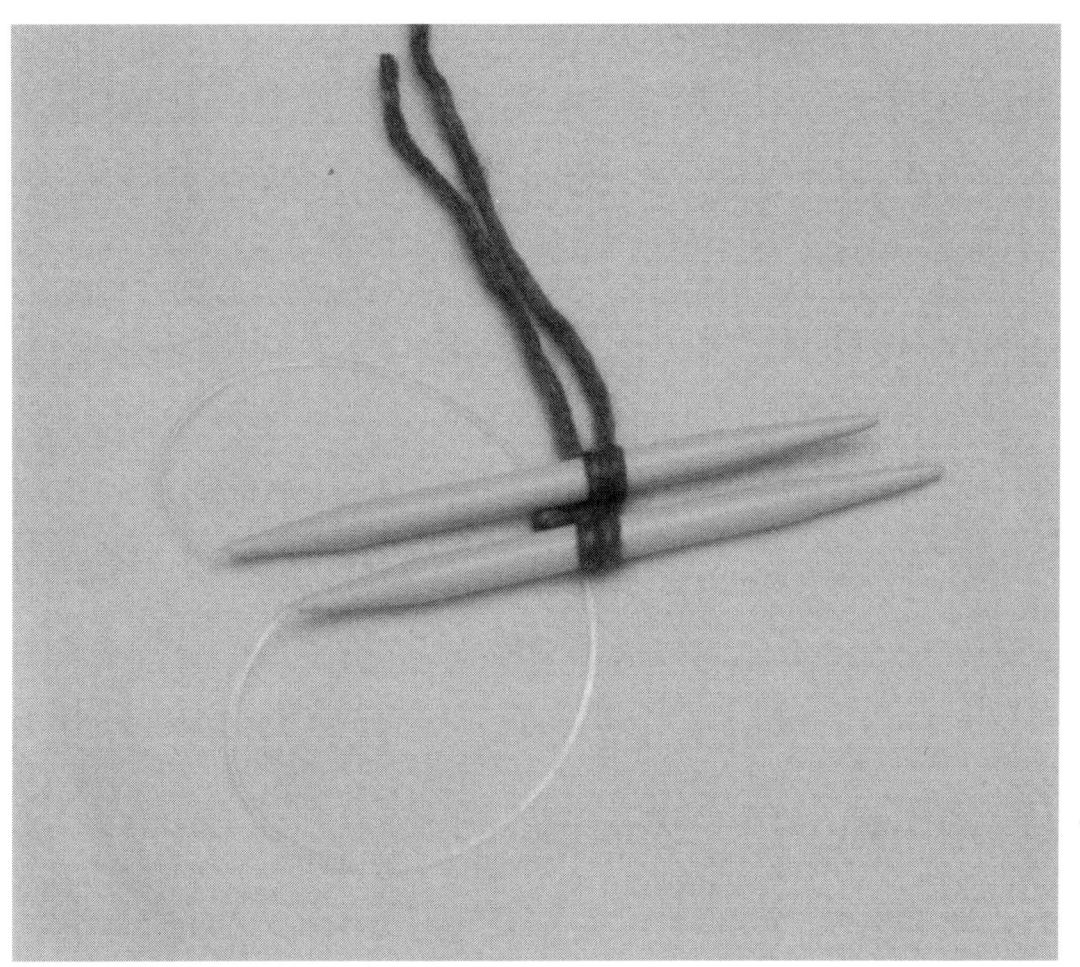

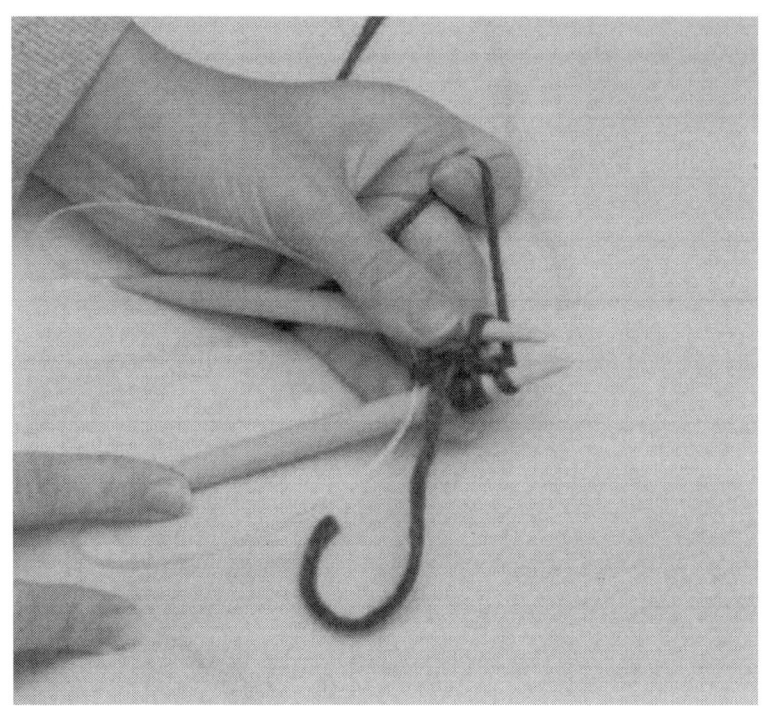

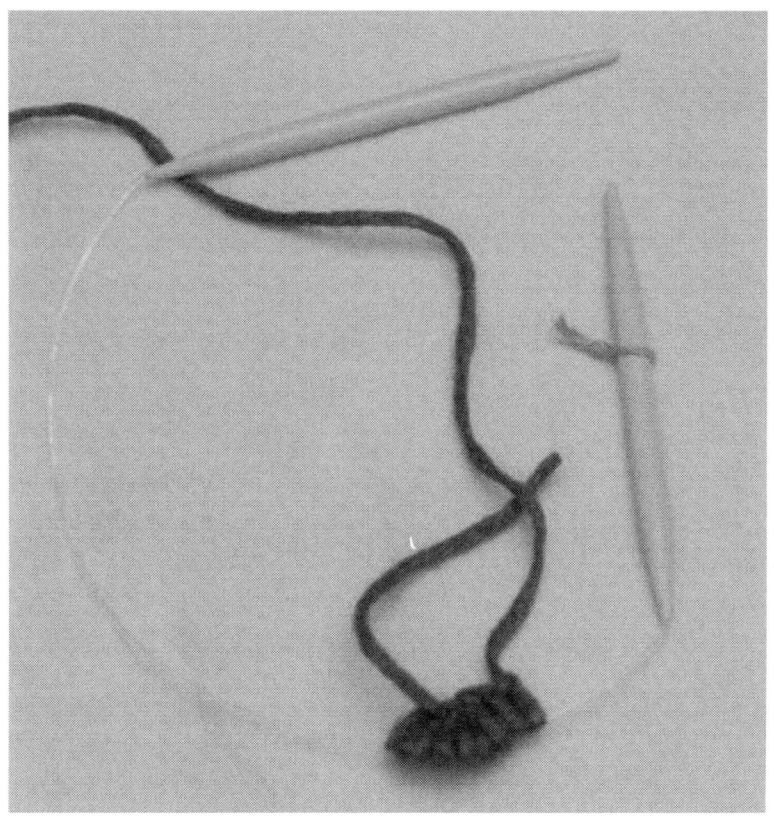

Row 2: double each second stitch

Row 3: double each third stitch

Repeat progressively like this up to 23 rows (or longer, as desired).

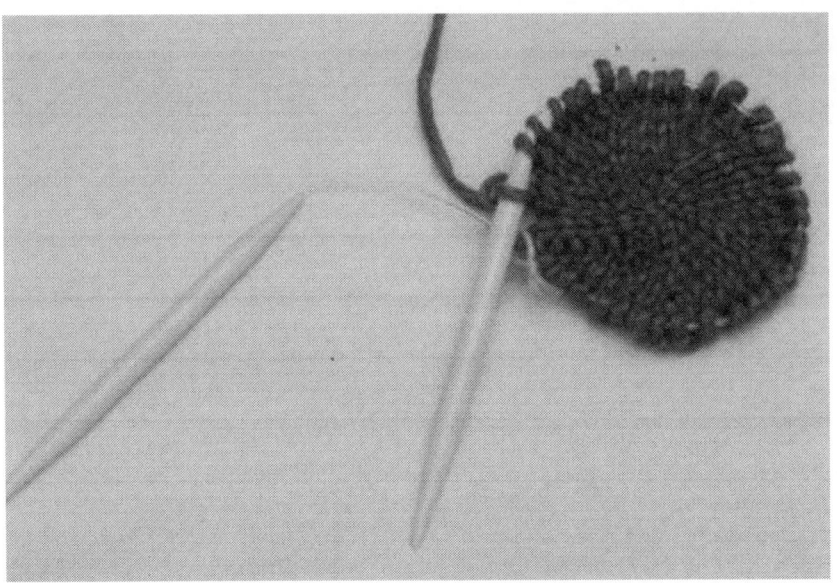

Start decreasing the stitches once you reach the size you need. You can do this by simply working two stitches into one. You have to decrease 5 stitches every round for about 10 rounds.

For the edge, work even for about 6 rounds alternating between a single purl stitch and a knit stitch.

Finish by casting off

2. DIY Finger Knit Rope Trivet

Tools and materials

Packing tape

10 yards of cotton sash cord

Instructions

With 8 inches of tail hanging, wrap your rope over the fore-finger, and around and under the middle finger. Wrap more thread around and below the fore finger, and bring it again around and under the middle finger. You should end up with two strands on either finger.

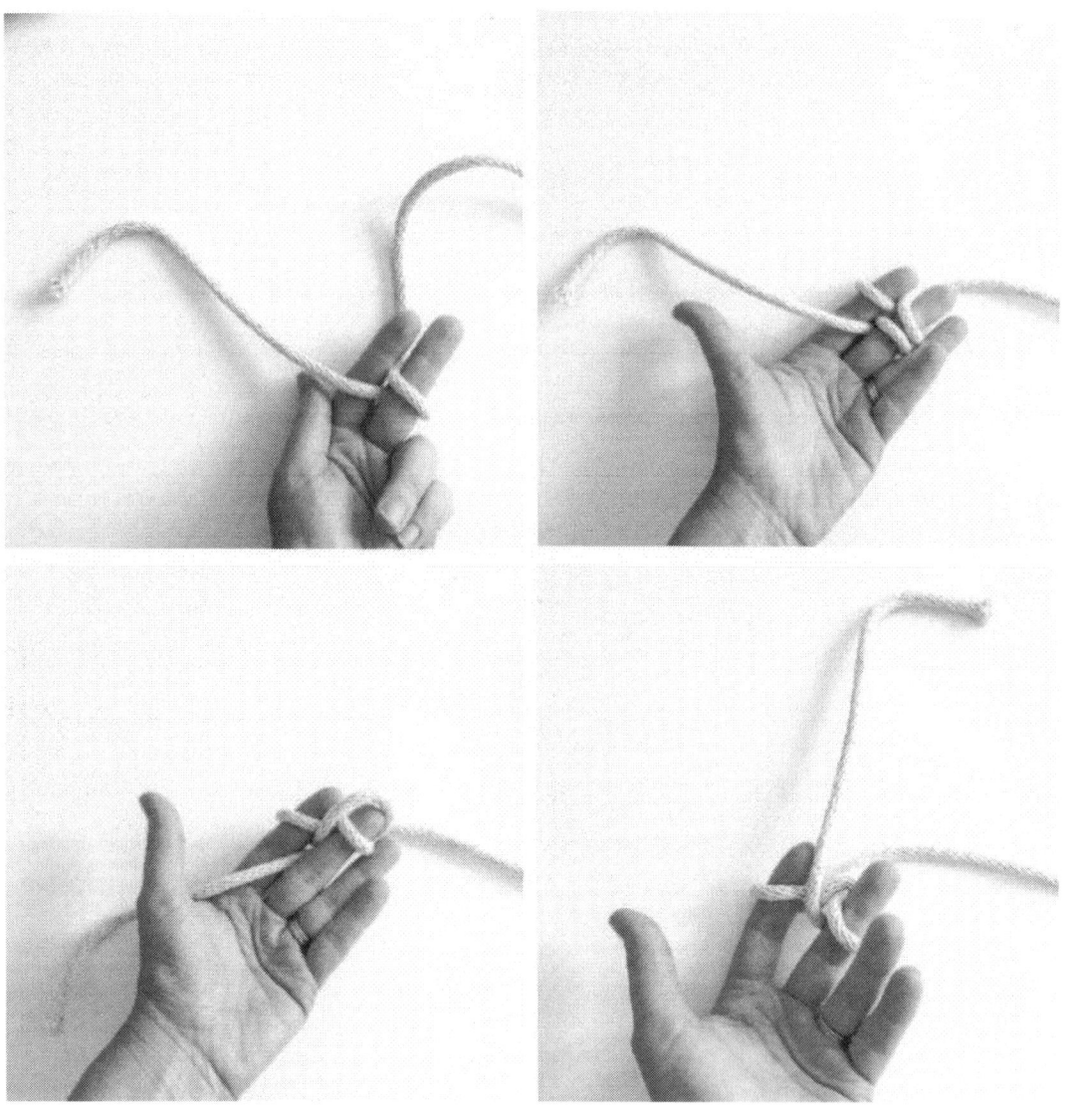

Raise the strand on the middle finger (bottom one) over the one on top, and pull it off of the middle finger.

Place the tail of rope in between the middle finger and fore finger.

Once again, wrap the thread around the middle finger, then bring it around and below the middle finger. Pull the middle finger thread over the upper one and slide it off of the middle finger. Pull the fore finger thread over the one on top and slide it off of the fore finger.

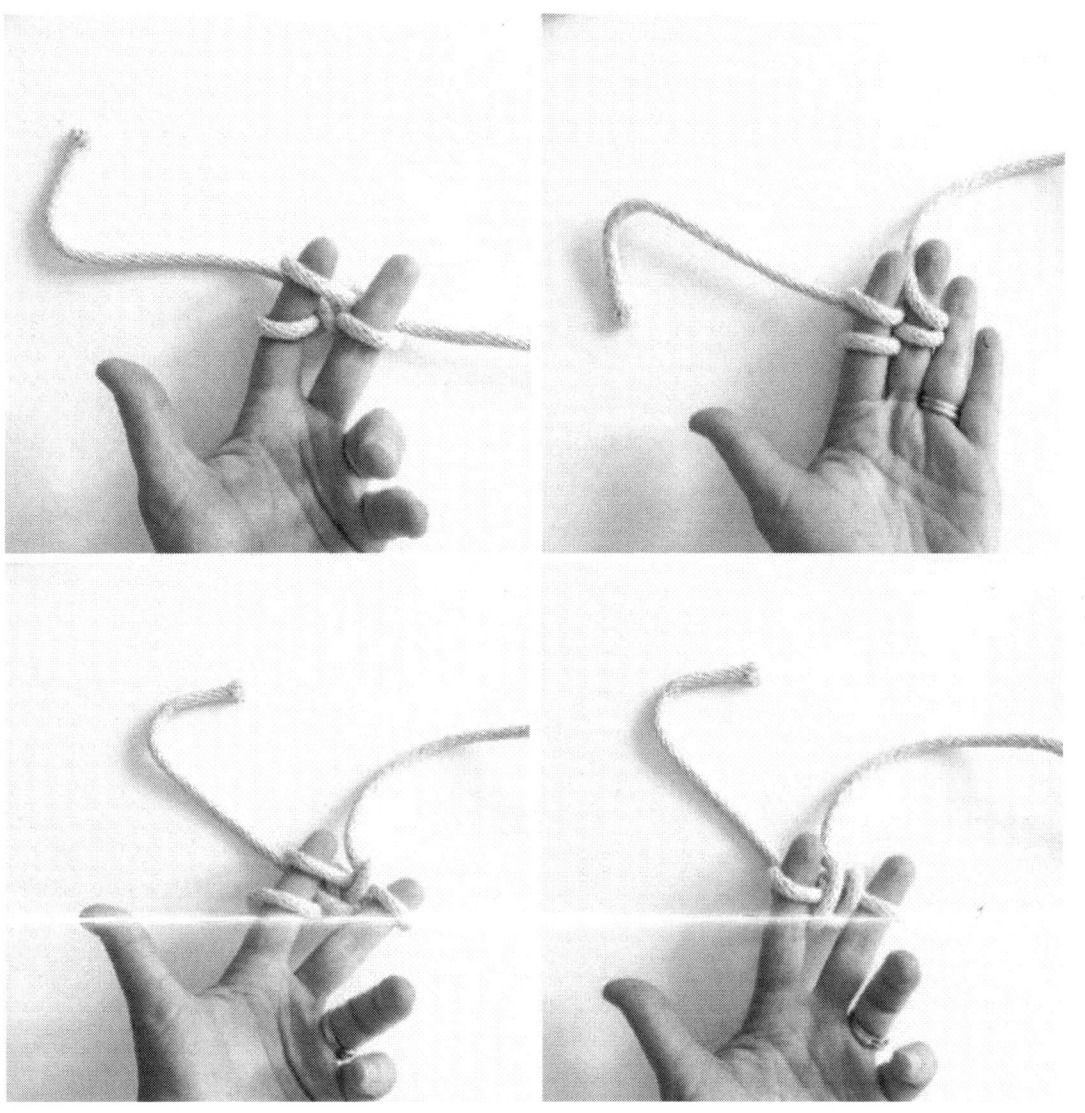

Finger knit about 55 rows using the four steps, then cut the end of your rope once you are done (after setting aside 1 ½ feet at the end). Bring the tail under the fore finger (under the loop), then pass it under the middle finger (below the loop). Tighten the end by pulling the loops from your fingers.

Slide the eight inches of tail through one thread from the 5th row, to start assembling the trivet. Pull until the thread starts coiling against itself.

Keep coiling the piece (with the thread flat) and passing the tail across the row directly facing its exit from the first coil. Tighten the thread to make the trivet coil around.

Slip the tail once more directly opposite its exit from the previous coil. Continue coiling and threading the tail until it makes it past the last coil, then tie the ends together into a knot and cut the rope.

3. Rib Ridge Dishcloth

Tools and materials

Pins and block mats

Regular stitch markers

Locking stitch markers

Scissors

Size 8 knitting needles

Instructions

CO 51 stitches

K 10 rows

1st row (right side): knit 7, purl 1, then knit and purl repeatedly to the last 7 stitches, knit 7

2nd row (wrong side): knit 8, then purl and knit repeatedly to the last 8 stitches, knit 8

3rd and 4th rows: K across the row

5th row: Knit 8, then purl and knit repeatedly to the last 8 stitches, knit 8

6th row: knit 7, then purl and knit repeatedly to the last 7 stitches, knit 7

7th and 8th rows: knit across the row

Start again from the 1st to the 8th row, repeating 7 times, and then finish the border edge by adding eight K rows. Cut your yarn and sew in the tails.

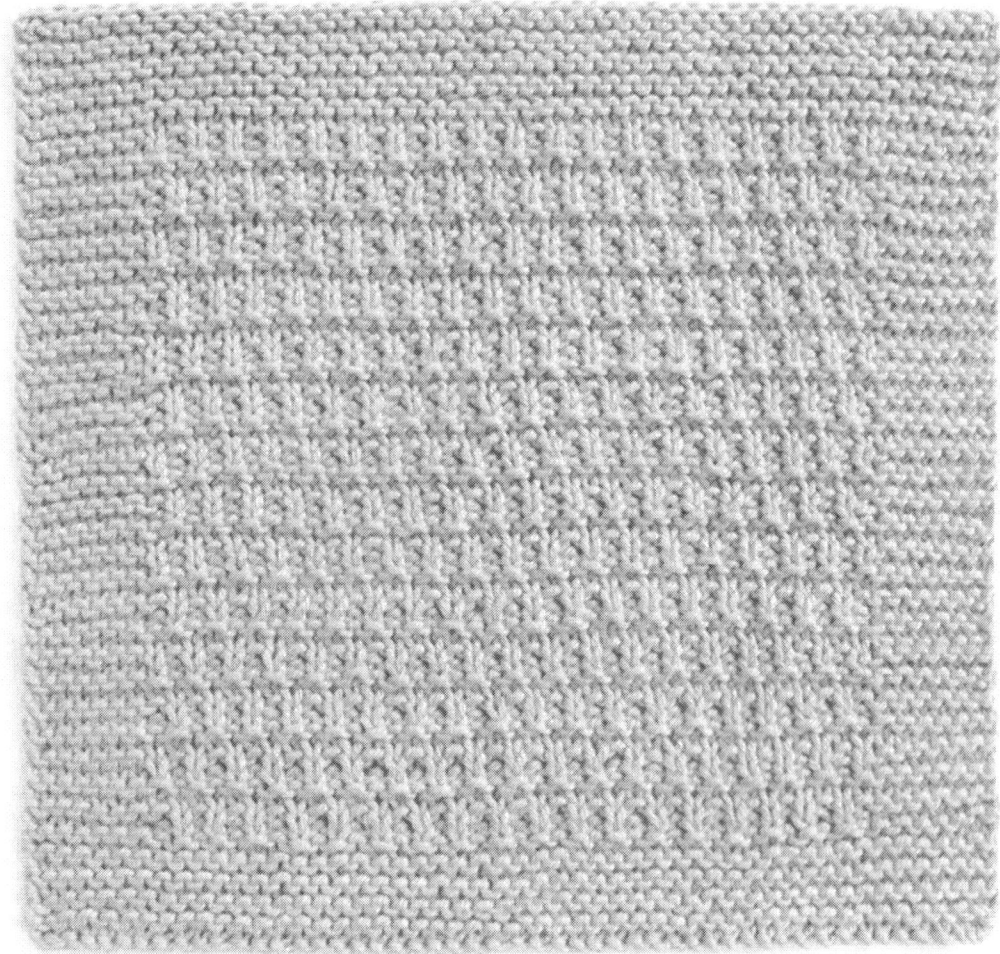

Gift Ideas

4. Toddler Slippers

Tools and materials

Size 8 straight needles

1 skein yarn

Instructions

Start by casting on 36 stitches. For the first 14 rows, knit using the garter stitch method, then cast off when starting the fifteenth row. This leaves you with 22 stitches. Cast off 14 stitches when starting the sixteenth row of the last 22 stitches so that 8 stitches are left at the center to knit the foot bed. Cast off when the foot bed is 4 ½ inches in size.

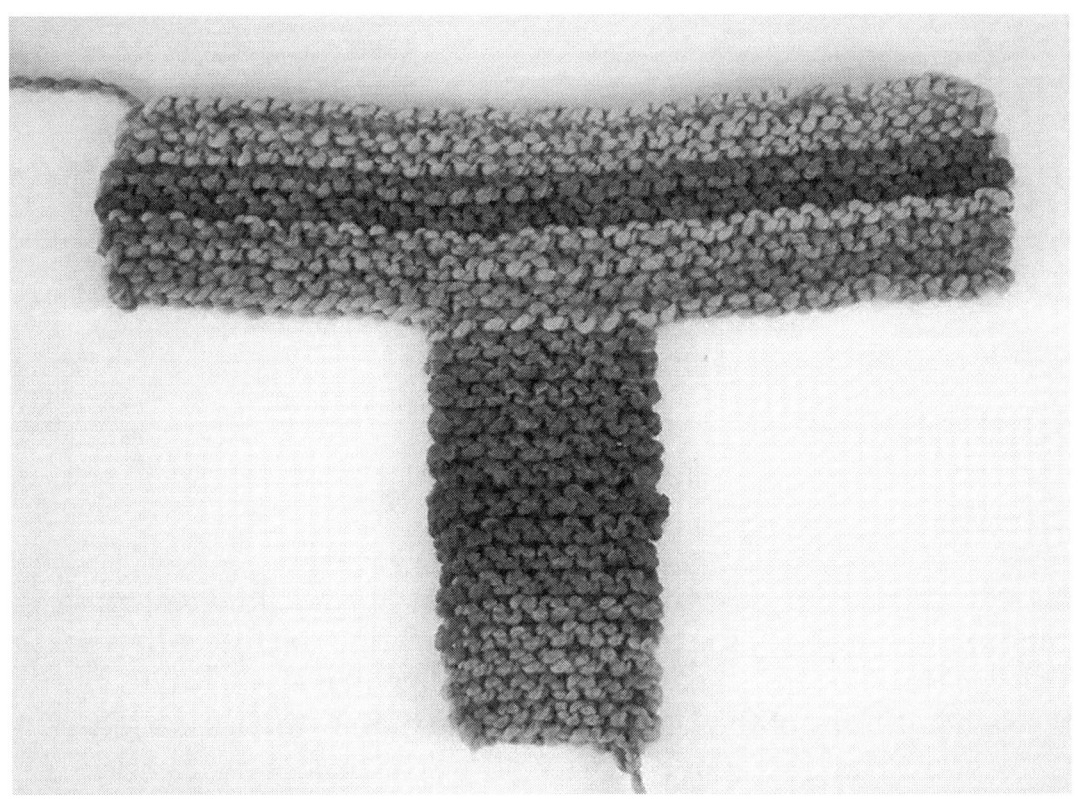

The finished piece should have a "T" shape, with the shorter side serving as the foot bed of the slipper and the longer part providing the sides and back heel. Fold one part of the longer side over the foot bed, then join at the bottom by sewing together.

Bring the second part over and join at the toes by sewing the parts together.

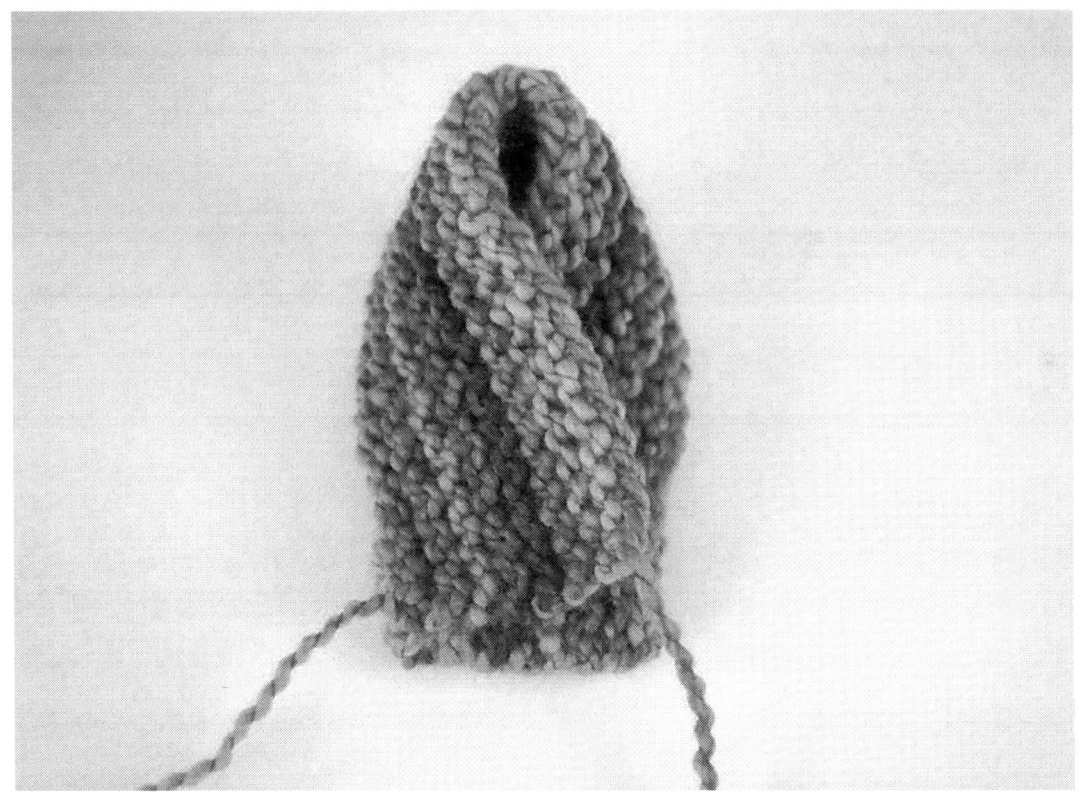

Place one end of the shorter side against the foot bed and sew the pieces together at the side. Do the same with the other part.

Repeat from step one for the second slipper, but join the sides to the foot bed in opposite directions this time.

5. Easy Knit Mittens

Tools and materials

Detachable stitch marker

Tape measure or ruler

Yarn needle

Yarn in two different colors (Yarn 1 and Yarn 2)

Size 7 circular knitting needles

Instructions

For the cuff:

CO 24 stitches using Yarn 1, then use the 2x2 rib stitch to knit 16 rows in the round

For the hand:

1st round: knit 3, then increase in the front and back. Repeat until you complete the round (30 sts in total)

2nd to 5th round: use the stockinette stitch to knit the rounds

6th round: knit 3, then place your stitch marker. Continue knitting until you complete the round

For the thumb gusset:

1st round: knit 1, increase once on the left, knit 1, increase once on the right, knit 1 (5 sts in total). Place your stitch marker and continue knitting using the stockinette stitch until you finish the round.

2nd and 3rd rounds: use the stockinette stitch to knit the rounds.

4th round: knit 1, increase once on the left, knit 3, increase on the right, knit 1 (7 sts in total). Place your stitch marker and continue knitting using the stockinette stitch to the end of the round.

8th and 9th round: use the stockinette stitch to knit the rounds.

Transfer the stitches for the thumb gusset onto some scrap yarn using tapestry or yarn needles, then secure.

For the top of hand:

CO 3 sts in place of the ones used for the thumb gusset, so that you now have 18 sts on one needle and 12 on the other.

Stitch 3 rows in the round using the stockinette stitch, then shift to Yarn 2 and continue stitching for 15 additional rounds.

For the Mitten top:

1st round: knit 3, then knit 2 stitches together. Repeat until you finish the round (24 sts in total)

2nd round: K all

3rd round: knit 2, then knit two stitches together. Repeat until you finish the round (18 sts left)

4th round: K all

5th round: knit 1, then knit two stitches together. Repeat until you finish the round (12 sts left)

6th round: K all

You should have 6 sts on each needle now. Seam and fasten off the stitches remaining.

For the thumb:

Mount the stitches for the thumb onto your circular needle and eliminate the scrap yarn.

Press the stitches onto your cord and knit 3 stitches into the gap using Yarn 1.

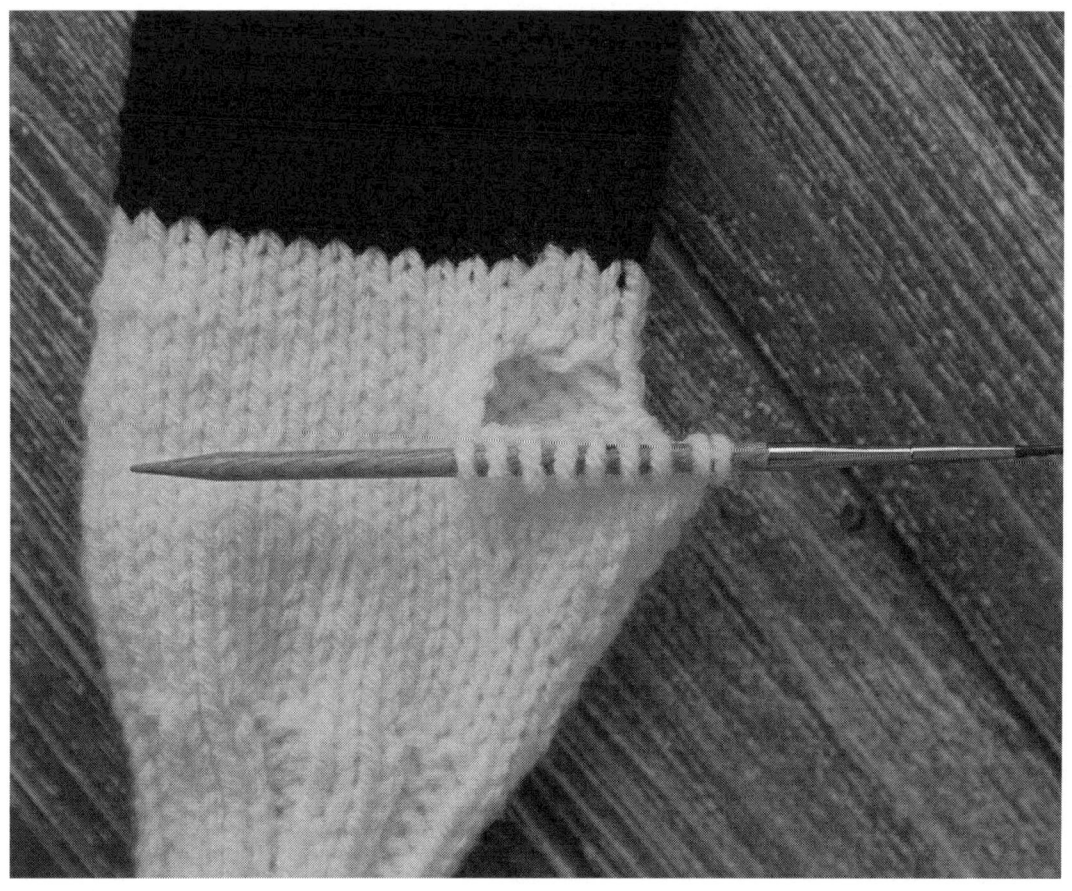

You should have 12 stitches in total; 9 on the one hand and 3 on the other. Knit 12 rows in the round using the stockinette stitch.

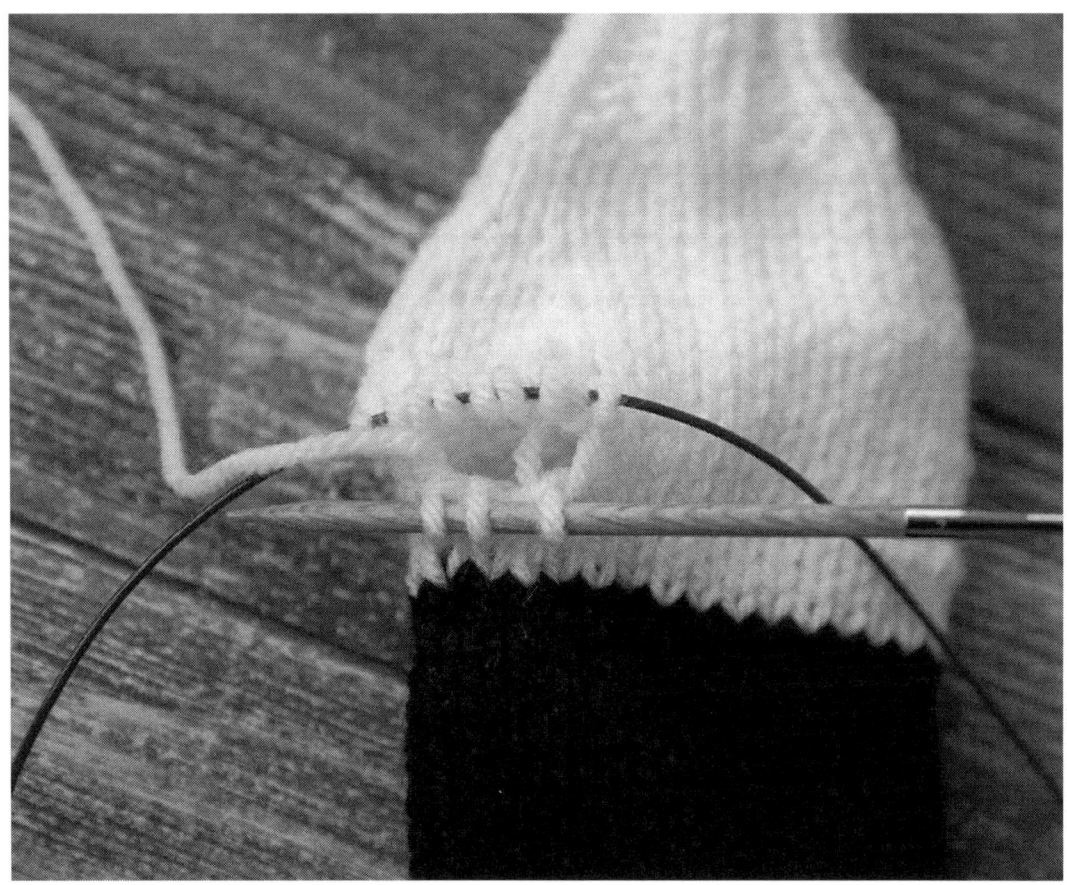

For the thumb top:

Rearrange the stitches to have 6 per needle

1st round: knit 1, then knit two stitches together. Repeat until you finish the round (8 sts left)

2nd round: K all

Each needle should now have 4 sts. Seam and fasten off the stitches remaining.

Finishing:

Turn the piece inside out and sew in all the ends.

Start from step one for the second mitten.

6. Child's Cat Hat

Tools and materials

Black, medium weight yarn (1 scrap)

Medium weight yarn (1 skein)

1 yarn needle

1 pair of scissors

1 tape measure

Size 7 DPNs

Instructions

CO 40 sts and mount them onto 3 DPNs. Work in the round.

Stitch for 1 inch using the 2x2 rib.

Continue ribbing using with stockinette stitch until the fabric is 4 inches in size from the beginning edge.

K6, K2tog, repeat to the end of the round.

K4 (35 stitches in total).

Knit one round.

K4, knit two together, repeat until you complete the round (25 stitches).

Knit one round.

K3, knit two together, repeat until you complete the round (20 stitches).

Knit one round.

K2, knit two together, repeat until you complete the round (15 stitches).

K1, knit two together, repeat until you complete the round (10 stitches).

Cut and thread the yarn through a yarn needle, then attach the stitches remaining. Close the top by pulling tight.

7. DIY Knit Basket

Tools and materials

7mm crochet hook

Size 19 circular knitting needles

1 skein yarn

Instructions

CO 32 stitches and knit 13 rounds.

K2tog throughout the 14th round (up to 16 sts).

K2tog throughout the 15th round (up to 8 sts).

Gently slide off the knitting needles, and pass the tail through the 8 stitches remaining. Pull gently.

Crochet a small trim over the top to make the basket stand up straight.

8. Heart Face Scrubby

Tools and materials

Tapestry needle

Measuring tape

Size 7 straight needles or circular needle

95 yards of yarn

Instructions

1st row: CO 17 stitches and turn

2nd to 5th row: knit 17 and turn

6th row: knit 3, purl 11, knit 3, then turn

7th row: knit 17, then turn

8th row: knit 3, purl 5, knit 1, purl 5, knit 3, then turn

9th row: knit 7, purl 3, knit 7, then turn

10th row: knit 3, purl 3, knit 5, purl 3, knit 3, then turn

11th row: knit 5, purl 7, knit 5, then turn

12th row: knit 3, purl 1, knit 9, pur1, knit 3, then turn

13th row: knit 4, purl 9, knit 4, then turn

14th row: knit 3, purl 1, knit 4, purl 1, knit 4, purl 1, knit 3, then turn

15th row: knit 4, purl 4, knit 1, purl 4, knit 4, then turn

16th row: knit 3, purl 2, knit 2, purl 3, knit 2, purl 2, knit 3, then turn

17th row: knit 17, then turn

18th row: knit 3, purl 11, knit 3, then turn

19th to 22nd rows: knit 17, then turn

23rd row: Cast off. Leave about 8 inches of tail, cut the yarn, then pull the tail through

Sew in the ends

9. Knitted Floor Pouf

Tools and materials

Trash bag

Bean bag filler

Sewing needle

Circular needles (size 15)

Thick yarn

Instructions

CO 35 sts and knit a rectangular piece about 3 foot long. Bind off.

Sew the rectangular piece together using spare yarn to end up with a huge "tube".

Slide your working needle through one loop at one side of the bottom end and thread it through to the other end, skipping every second loop. Seal the bottom together by pulling the thread of yarn tightly.

The piece should have a basket-like shape at this point. Add bean bag filler into your trash bag, and then insert the bag into the basket.

Seal the top using the same method used for the bottom part.

10. Hand-knit Straight Tie

Tools and materials

Scissors

Tapestry needle

Size 5 straight needles

Different colors of wool yarn (2 skeins)

Instructions

CO 11 sts with Yarn A

Knit 21 inches using the seed stitch

K2tog on the front and back to decrease to nine stitches

Knit 1 inch using the seed stitch

P2tog on the front and back to decrease to seven stitches

Knit 10 inches using the seed stitch

Change to Yarn B and continue stitching with the seed stitch for 22-24 inches

Bind off and sew in the ends

For the Keeper Loop:

CO 11 sts using Yarn A

Knit 1 inch using the seed stitch

Bind off without weaving in the ends

Join to the tie using your tapestry needle and yarn tails

Scarves

11. Garter Stitch Scarf

Tools and materials

Super bulky yarn (100-200 yards)

Scissors

Crochet hook (9mm) for sewing in the ends

Size 13 knitting needles

Instructions

CO 12 stitches (more or less, depending on your desired length).

Using the garter stitch method, knit all the stitches across every row until you achieve the length you want or until you are left with about one yard of yarn.

You may also add more yarn if you need to incorporate a different color or to simply extend the length of your scarf.

Cast off the stitches and cut the yarn, being sure to leave about six inches of tail behind.

Finish by weaving in the ends using your crochet hook.

12. Ionos Infinity Scarf

Tools and materials

Optional: tapestry needle

Size 6 circular needle

Light yarn

Instructions

Cast on 96 stitches

1st row (right side): K

2nd row (wrong side): P

Repeat the two rows once.

1st eyelet row (right side): knit 2, (yarn over, knit two together, repeat to the last two stitches), knit 2.

Next row (wrong side): purl, then knit in stockinette stitch for 10 rows.

2nd eyelet row (right side): knit 2, (knit two together, yarn over, repeat to the last two stitches), knit 2.

Repeat from the first eyelet row 15 times more.

Additional eyelet row (right side): knit 2, (yarn over, knit two together, repeat to the last two stitches), knit 2.

Next row (wrong side): purl.

Knit in the stockinette stitch for 6 rows.

Graft together the ends using your tapestry needle.

13. One Row Handspun Scarf

Tools and materials

5mm needles

Worsted weight yarn

Instructions

CO 26 sts

1st row: k2, knit into the subsequent stitch from the back, p1, repeat to the last two stitches, k2.

Repeat 1st row until you reach the desired size of your scarf, then bind off.

Blankets And Throws

14. Simple Blanket

Tools and materials

Size 19 knitting needles

Wool yarn

Instructions

Start by leaving a tail of wool from your yarn, then form a slipknot about ten inches from the end of this tail. Use the tail to create a little loop. Bring and pull the big yarn across this loop.

Slide one needle through the slipknot loop and hold it with your right hand. Grab the yarn and wrap it around the left hand. Pass the needle across the loop around your thumb, then release to form a stitch on the needle. Proceed by casting on fourteen stitches (to produce a 7.5 inch square).

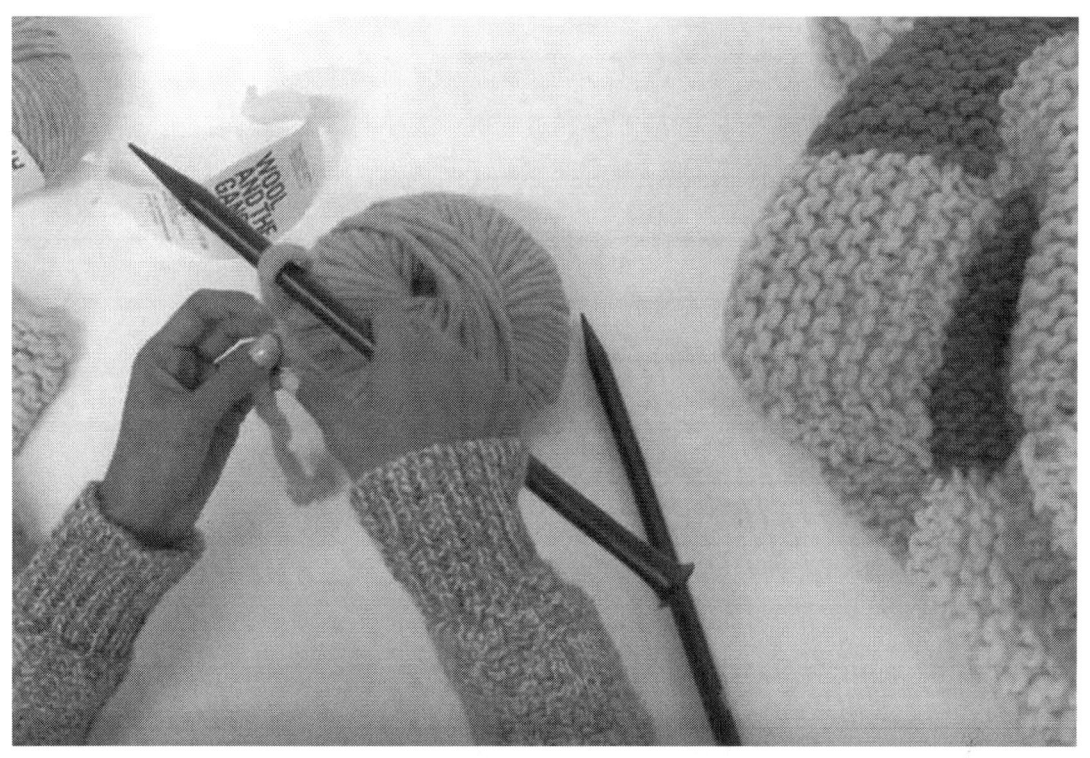

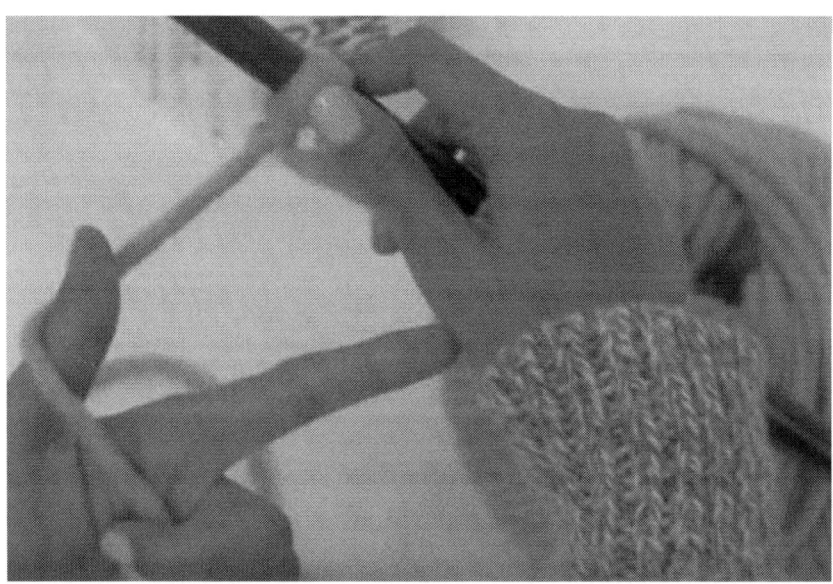

Knit-stitch one row with your right hand (empty) needle.

Knit some more to expand your square up to 7.5" in height.

Bind off. Knit 2 stitches, then pull stitch 1 over stitch 2 using the needle on your left hand. This will leave you with only one stitch on the right side. Leave some tail (about 30cm) before cutting the yarn, then pull the thread through to complete your square.

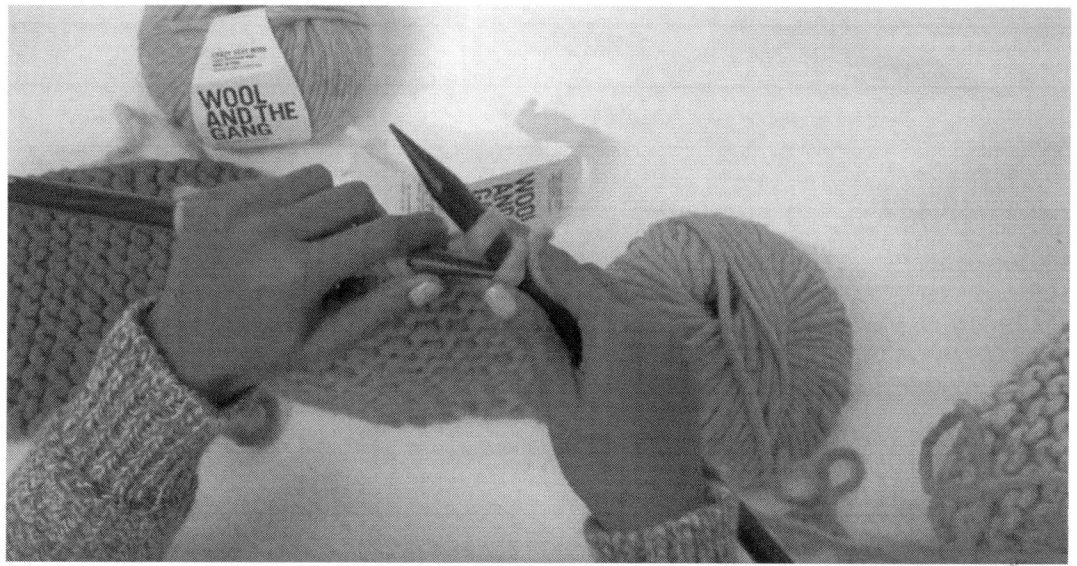

Weave the squares together using a sewing needle, passing it through the small "bumps" at the edges.

15. Sunny Baby Blanket

Tools and materials

Size 8 circular needles

4 skeins yarn

Instructions

For the blanket:

CO 132 stitches

$1^{st} - 16^{th}$ rows: knit

The pattern:

1st row: knit (right side

2nd row: k8 (p8,k4) nine times, p8, k8

Odd rows (3 to 11): repeat the first row

Even rows (4 to 12): repeat the second row

13th to 18th rows: knit

Restart the pattern from the first to last row 11 more times, then repeat the 1st to 12th rows

Cast off

16. Double Seed Stitch Blanket

Tools and materials

Size 13 circular needles

6 skeins yarn

Instructions

CO 77 sts

1st row (wrong side): knit 1, purl 1, repeat to the last stitch, knit 1

2nd row (right side): repeat first row

3rd row (wrong side): purl 1, knit 1, repeat to the last stitch, purl 1

4th row (right side): repeat the third row

Restart steps from the first row until you achieve desired length

Cast off and sew in the ends

Shawls

17. Quick and Easy Shawl

Tools and materials

Circular knitting needle (size 10 1/2)

7 balls of yarn

Instructions

CO 139 stitches

Knit using garter stitch for three rows, with the first row being wrong side

4th row (right side): knit 1, knit two together, knit to the last three stitches, knit two together, knit 1

5th row: knit

Repeat 4th and 5th rows to the last 69 stitches

Bind off three stitches beginning every row to the last three stitches

Next row: knit three together and fasten off

18. Easy Lace Shawl

Tools and materials

Size 10 knitting needles

3 balls of yarn

Instructions

Holding two strands together, CO 61 stitches

Purl one row

1st row (right side): knit1, [*(yarn over, slip1, knit1, pass the slipped st over, repeat), knit1, (knit two together, yarn over, repeat), knit1] repeat

2nd row: purl

3rd row: knit2, (yarn over, slip1, knit1, pass the slipped st over, yarn over, slip1, knit two together, pass the slipped st over, yarn over, knit two together, yarn over, knit three; repeat to the last nine stitches), yarn over, slip1, knit1, pass the slipped st over, yarn over, slip one, knit two together, pass the slipped st over, yarn over, knit two together, yarn over, knit2

4th row: purl

Restart from the first row to the fourth row until you're 54 inches from the beginning. Cast off.

19. Xcellent Shawl

Tools and materials

Size 9 circular needles

Yarn

Blocking wires

Instructions

Body:

Cast on six stitches

- 1st row (right side): (knit 1 twice around the needle, repeat), yarn over, knit to the last two stitches, yarn over, (knit 1 twice around the needle; repeat), + two stitches (8 in total).
- 2nd row (wrong side): knit 2, (knit 1, yarn over, knit 1) in subsequent stitch, knit to the last three stitches, (knit 1, yarn over, knit 1) in subsequent stitch, knit 2; + four stitches (12 in total).
- 3rd to 18th row: repeat the first and second rows eight times more; + forty-eight stitches (60 in total).
- 19th row: (knit 1 twice around the needle, repeat), yarn over, knit four times around the needle to the last two stitches, yarn over, (knit 1 twice around the needle, repeat); + two stitches (62 in total).
- 20th row: knit 2, (knit 1, yarn over, knit 1) in the subsequent stitch.

- Remove and slide the next four elongated stitches onto the needle on your right. Without changing the order, slip these stitches back to the needle on your left over the stitches that have not been worked. Remove and work the next four elongated stitches on the needle on your left, then knit the ones you had slipped. Do this up to the last three stitches, then (knit 1, yarn over, knit 1) in the subsequent stitch, knit 2; + four stitches (66 in total).
- Repeat the 5th – 20th rows twice; 162 stitches
- Repeat the 5th – 19th rows once; 206 stitches
- 68th row: knit 3, repeat step (F) up to the last three stitches, knit 3

Hem:

69th row: (knit 1 twice around the needle, repeat), knit 1 (knit 2, knit two together, yarn over three times, pass the slipped stitch over, knit 2, repeat up to the last three stitches), knit 1, (knit 1 twice around the needle, repeat); 231 stitches.

70th row: knit 2, M9, purl 2, purl two together, (unwind yarn overs then M9, purl 2, knit two together, purl 2, repeat to the last nine stitches, unwind yarn overs then M9, purl 2, knit two together, M9, knit 2; total of 378 stitches.

Cast off purl-wise

Finishing:

Make a straight edge over the top using your blocking wire, then pin out the hem's waves in a curve.

Headbands

20. Cable Headbands

Tools and materials

Size 11 needles

1 ball of bulky yarn

Instructions

Make one stitch, then slide the next 3 sts onto a 6-inch DPN (bamboo) in the front.

Resume knitting on the main row, behind the bamboo needle.

Work in three stitches.

Slip these stitches onto the right sided bamboo needle, then twist slightly to make it easier to knit the stitches onto the main (working) needle. Continue knitting until all the stitches are on the main needle.

Drop the short needle and knit the row regularly until you reach row 7 requiring the left cable.

Knit seven stitches and slip the next three onto your bamboo needle, with the needle staying at the back this time. Knit 3 sts using your working needles, so that only one stitch is left on the main needle.

Again, slip the stitches onto the right side, with the bamboo needle coming forward so that you can work the stitches out of the needle.

Knit the last stitch using your working needles.

21. Newbie Knitted Headband

Tools and materials

Darning needle

Wool yarn

Instructions

Start by creating a slipknot, then leave about 4 inches of tail hanging to be used at the end of the project.

CO 12 stitches (or more for a wider headband).

Knit all the rows using the garter stitch method until you are able to wrap the garment comfortably around your head. Aim for a width that is slightly tight, as the band is prone to become loose over time.

Bind off your stitches once you have achieved the desired width for your headband. Leave behind about three arm's length of tail for sewing or seaming together the piece.

Pass the tail through a tapestry or darning needle, then seam together by joining the cast off edge and the cast on edge of the knitted piece.

22. Seed Stitch Headband

Tools and materials

Size 4 knitting needles

Yarn

Instructions

CO 15 stitches then knit using the moss stitch until the piece is large enough to fit around your head.

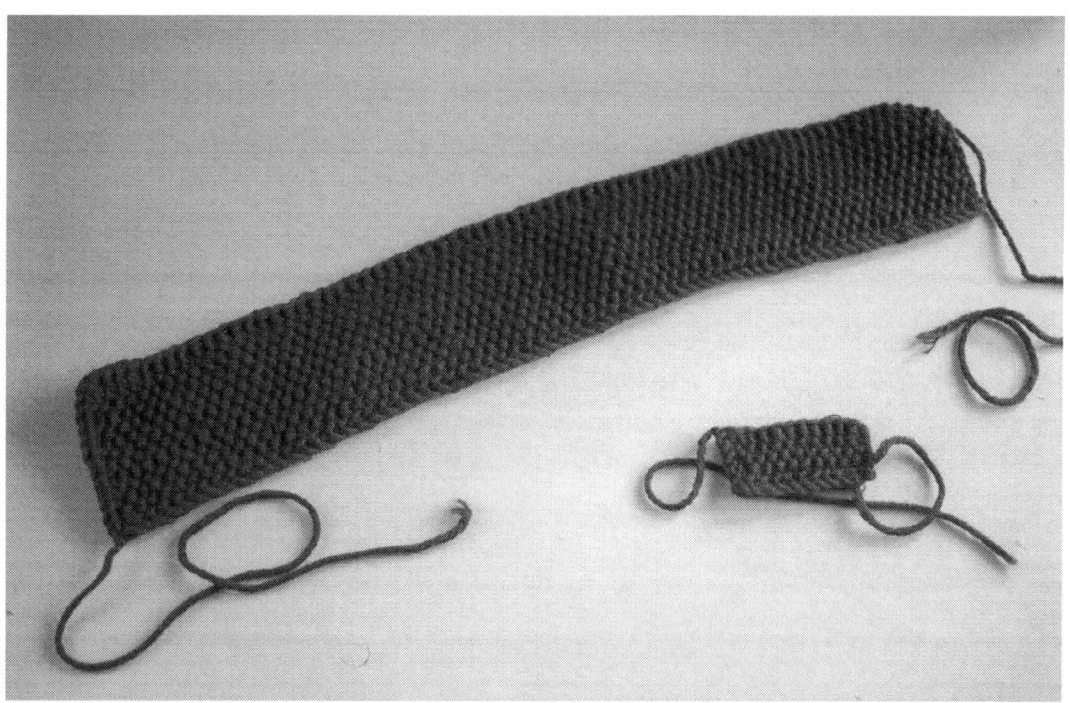

Bind off, but don't weave in the tails.

Join the ends together using one of the hanging tails.

CO 7 stitches for the ribbon and knit again using the moss stitch method until you reach the right length.

Join the ribbon to the headband and sew the pieces together using one of the hanging tails.

Finish by sewing all the threads remaining.

Cowls

23. Ribbed Velvet Knit Cowl

Tools and materials

Measuring tape

Yarn needle

Scissors

Size 10 circular knitting needles

2 skeins yarn

Special abbreviations

PFB = increase by purling in the front and back

Instructions

Cast on 97 stitches using two strands

Proceed with the 1x1 rib

1st row: k1, p1, then repeat until you are left with one stitch, k1

2nd row: p1, k1, then repeat until you are left with one stitch, p1

Continue alternating between the 1st and 2nd rows until your piece is about nine inches from the starting end, then end with a row containing an even number of stitches.

Subsequent row: k1 then PFB (purl front back), knit three stitches together until you are left with one stitch.

Continue with the 1x2 rib

Subsequent row: p1, k2, then repeat until you are left with one stitch, p1

1st row: k1, p2, then repeat until you are left with one stitch, k1

2nd row: p1, k2, then repeat until you are left with one stitch, p1

Continue alternating the first and second rows until your piece is about fifteen inches from the starting end, then end with an even row.

Bind off loosely and set aside a long tail before you cut your yarn.

The cowl:

Spread out the piece with the 1x2 ribbed side facing up and the odd-rowed part at the top.

Bring the two edges together by folding the piece in half, so that the odd side is within the fold and the even side is facing outward.

Join both sides using yarn needle and the reserved long tail to create your cowl.

24. Seed Stitch Cowl

Tools and materials

Stitch marker

Measuring tape or ruler

Blunt tapestry needle or large yarn needle

Scissors

Circular knitting needle (size 11)

Super bulky yarn (about 175 yards)

Instructions

Create and place a slipknot on your left needle. Slide the needle on your right through the slipknot, then start knitting without removing the slipknot from your left needle. Stretch and lift up the loop on your right, then slip it onto the needle on your left.

Knit through the next stitch without un-mounting the old one from the needle on your left.

Stretch and lift the loop on the needle on your right, then slip it onto the needle on your left.

Repeat the last two steps until you have enough stitches casted on.

CO 68 stitches then place a stitch marker on your working needle. Place this needle on your right hand and the other on your left. Knit in the round, being careful not to twist the casted-on end.

1ˢᵗ round: knit 1, purl 1 in the round. Place stitch marker.

2ⁿᵈ round: purl 1, knit 1 in the round. Place stitch marker.

Repeat the first and second rounds until the piece is 12 inches high.

Remove the stitch marker and loosely cast off all the stitches.

For the finishing:

Cut the yarn, leaving a tail of about 6-8 inches in length. Pull the tail through the last loop and thread it through the yarn needle.

Identify the loop for the first casted-off stitch, which should be laying on the cast-off edge, then pass the yarn needle through it under both strands, from front to back.

Pass the needle through the last casted-off stitch to join the bind off, then tie a knot at the back of your project. Weave in all the tails remaining.

25. Beginner Knit Cowl

Tools and materials

Measuring tape

Scissors

Tapestry needle

About 245 yards of yarn

Straight knitting needles (size 10.5)

Instructions

Cast on 35 stitches

1st row: knit all stitches

Repeat the first row until you are about 36" from the beginning.

Bind off all stitches, leaving about 18 to 24 inches of yarn tail.

Using the whip stitch, seam together the edges with the remaining tail.

Weave in the ends.

Seasonal Projects

Summer

26. Big Loop Knitted Hat

Tools and materials

Big loop yarn (approximately 36m)

Size 19 needles

Instructions

1st round: CO 18 stitches. You need about 3m of yarn to cast on. Avoid pulling too tight during this step, as it is important to leave some space for this yarn to be able to breathe. A general rule of thumb is to knit fairly loosely, especially since the needles you are using are relatively small for yarn of this size. Keep in mind that you may need more yarn if you decide to use larger needles, such as the size 36 set.

2nd to 10th rounds: knit

11th round: knit two stitches together (so that you are left with nine on the needles when you're done).

Leave behind about 15cm of tail then cut the yarn and bring it across the loops. Tighten by pulling.

Finish by casting on the reserved tail of yarn to the inside of the completed piece, then tie it up with a knot.

27. Chunky Knit Boot Cuffs

Tools and materials

Large yarn needle

Super bulky yarn

Knitting needles (size 13)

Instructions

CO 28 sts

1st to 8th rows: k2, p2

9th to 16th rows: switch to the stockinette stitch

Leave about 12 inches of tail then bind off.

Sew together the short ends using your yarn needle.

Turn the right side out, then repeat from the beginning to make the second cuff.

28. Chunky Yarn Knitted Pillow Case

Tools and materials

Size 50 needle

Yarn

Instructions

First side:

CO 11 stitches

1st row: knit, then purl, then knit, then purl, the knit, then purl, then knit, then purl, then knit, then purl and then knit.

2nd row: purl, then knit, then purl, then knit, then purl, then knit, then purl, knit, then purl, then knit, and then purl.

Repeat the first and second rows up to the eleventh row.

Second side:

Repeat the pattern for the first side.

Once you are done with the two parts, sew three sides together, then insert your cushion before sewing the last side.

Winter

29. Easy Knit Baby Hat

Tools and materials

Scissors

Yarn needle

Size 13 DPNs

Size 13 circular knitting needles

Instructions

For the band:

1st round: CO 36, then k1, p1 repeatedly to the end

2nd round: k1, p1, then repeat to the end

Repeat the second round 5 times more

For the sides:

K all stitches

Repeat ten times more

For the crown:

1st round: k4, knit two stitches together, then repeat for 40 stitches

2nd round: k3, knit two stitches together, then repeat to the end (32 stitches)

3rd round: k2, knit two stitches together, then repeat to the end (24 stitches)

4th round: k1, knit two stitches together, then repeat to the end (16 stitches)

5th round: knit two stitches together, then repeat to the end (8 stitches)

Finishing:

Leave an eight-inch tail, then cast off. Pass the tail across the stitches remaining using a yarn needle, and sew in the ends after securing the opening.

30. Easy Arm Warmers

Tools and materials

Scissors

Darning needle

Tape measure

Knitting needles (size 8)

Yarn

Instructions

Cast on 26 stitches

Purl two rows

Knit two rows

Repeat the last two steps 5 times

Purl two rows

Knit in the stockinette stitch for four rows (beginning with a knit row)

Purl two rows

Knit in the stockinette stitch for four rows

Purl two rows

Knit in the stockinette stitch for four rows

Purl two rows

Knit in the stockinette stitch for four rows

Purl two rows

Knit to the end of row

Purl three rows

Knit to the end of row

Purl three rows

Knit two rows

Purl two rows

Knit two rows

Purl two rows

Bind off and weave in the ends

31. Garter Wrist Warmers

Tools and materials

6 blunt needles

Size 13 knitting needles

Yarn

Instructions

CO 17 sts. Using the garter stitch method, knit about 7.5 inches from the start, then cast off with approximately 18 inches of tail hanging.

Pass the tail through the blunt needle and sew together the bounded-on edge and the casted-off edge. Weave in the loose ends.

Spring

32. Felted Cloche

Tools and materials

Size 9 circular needles

Size 9 DPNs

2 balls (about 365 yards) of yarn

Instructions

CO 100 stitches using circular needles or DPNs (double pointed needles), and mark the start of the first round.

Alternative 1: use the garter stitch method for up to 2.5 inches of your work to get a flat brim.

Alternative 2: use the stockinette stitch method for up to 2.5 inches of your work to get a rolled brim.

Subsequent row: k3, knit two stitches together in the round until you are left with 80 stitches, then start knitting the stockinette stitch until you expand the piece to 8.5 inches.

Crown shaping:

1st row: k8, knit two stitches together in the round

2nd and 3rd rows: k in the round

4th row: k7, then knit two stitches together in the round

5th and 6th rows: k in the round

7th row: k6, then knit two together in the round

8th row: k in the round

9th row: k5, then knit two together in the round

10th row: k in the round

11th row: k4, then knit two in the round

12th row: k in the round

13th row: k3, then knit two together in the round

14th row: k2, then knit two together in the round

15th row: k1, then knit two together in the round

16th row: knit two together in the round, then cut the yarn and thread the tail through the last eight stitches. Sew in the ends.

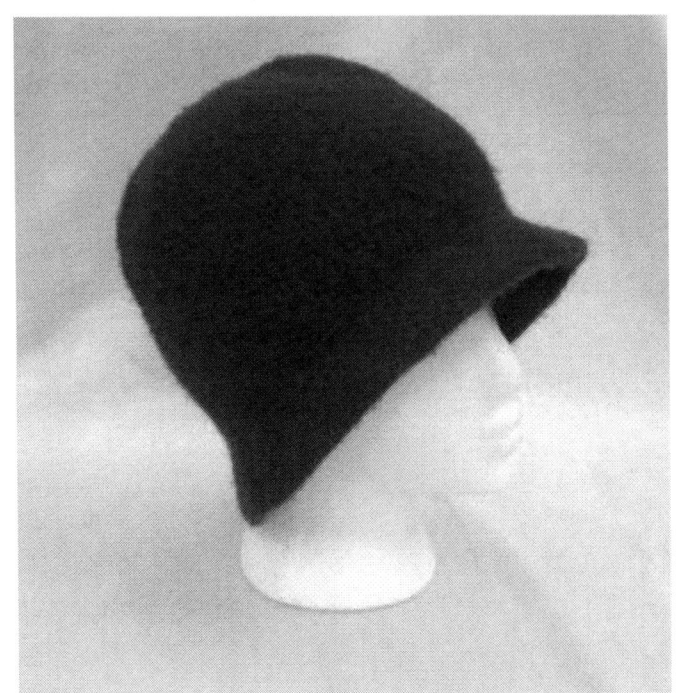

33. Simple Garter Stitch Knit Cowl

Tools and materials

Tapestry needle (for weaving in the ends)

Stitch marker

Circular knitting needles (12.75mm)

2 skeins yarn

Instructions

Cast on 60 stitches and work in the round without twisting. Place a stitch marker

1st row: purl to the end

2nd row: knit to the end

3rd row: purl

Repeat the second and third rows until you are about 7.5 inches from the beginning.

Following row: knit one, then increase (k1 in the front and back) to the end.

Repeat the first and second rows until your fabric is about 15 inches in size, then loosely cast off.

Weave in the ends.

34. Color Blocked Afghan

Tools and materials

Yarn size 17 circular knitting needles

Instructions

NB: you need to work with two strands (held as one) when knitting this blanket.

CO the required stitches, depending on the projected size of your blanket.

Knit in the garter stitch method until you are about a fifth of the required length of the finished project, then change colors. Continue knitting, changing colors every fifth of the way until you have five knitted stripes.

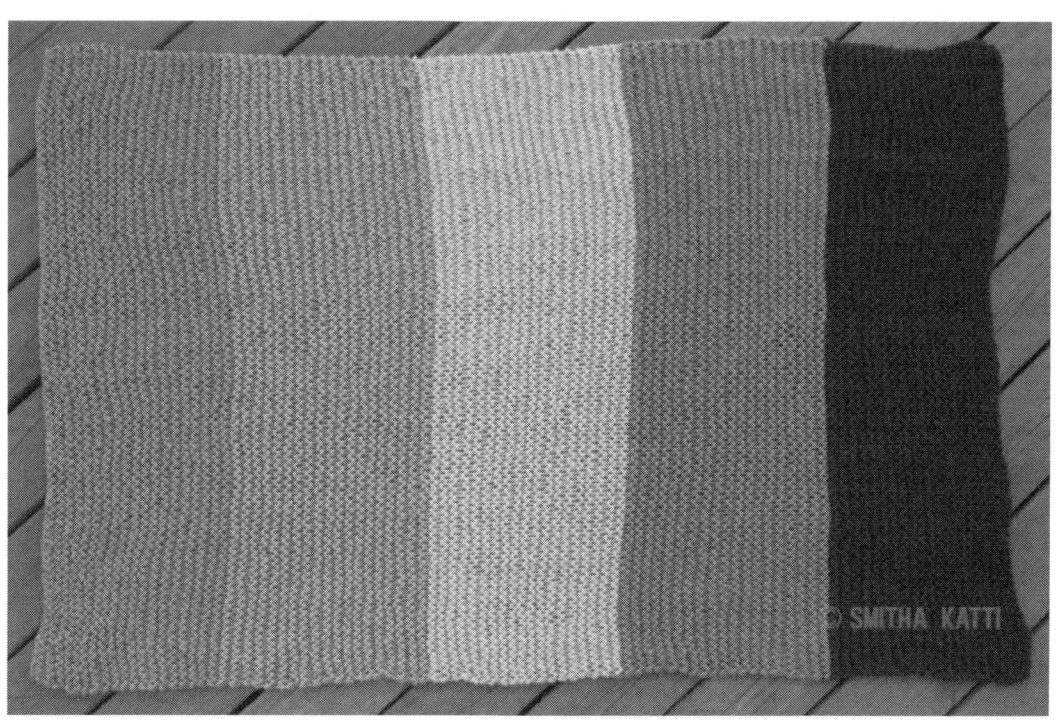

Autumn

35. Knit Hat Pattern

Tools and materials

Size 10 circular knitting needles

Size 6 circular knitting needles

1 skein yarn

Instructions

Cast on 89 stitches, place your stitch marker, and join together without twisting the stitches.

Knit 1, purl 1, repeat until you reach the fifth round.

Using your circular knitting needles, knit 1, purl 1 repeatedly for eight inches.

Start decreasing: knit 1, knit two together, repeat until you complete the round.

Next round: knit until you complete the round.

Knit two together, repeat until you complete the round.

Cut the yarn then thread across the stitches remaining. Secure

Sew in the ends.

Create and add a pom over the hat, then stitch it tightly into place.

36. Knitted Pumpkin Pattern

Tools and materials

Toy stuffing

Scissors

Darning needle

Tape measure

Size 6 knitting needles (circular)

8 ply light worsted/brown yarn

8 ply light worsted/orange yarn

Instructions

CO 36 sts, with about 15 inches of tail hanging

Using your circular knitting needles, join the stitches together without twisting.

Knit 5, purl 1, repeat for three inches

Cut the yarn then thread across the stitches remaining. Pull tight and tie together with a knot.

Fill the toy stuffing into the pumpkin, with the right side turned out, until it's full and round.

Thread the yarn out through the open end and seal the opening by pulling tight. Tie the yarn into a knot to seal.

Slide the 15 inches of tail left at the beginning through the other end so that two threads are hanging from one side.

Tie the threads together then wrap them around until you have a pumpkin shape. Tie the yarn into a knot to maintain the shape.

Sew in the ends

Use the brown yarn and needles to knit the stalk flat: start by casting on eight stitches, then knit one row. Continue knitting in the stockinette stitch until you are fifteen inches from the beginning.

Bind off then knit over the pumpkin piece.

37. Maple Leaf

Tools and materials

Wool needle

Yarn in fall/autumn colors

Knitting needles

Instructions

CO 10 stitches

1st row: k2tog, k to the last two stitches, k2tog (eight stitches)

2nd row: K

Repeat the first and second row

4th row: K

5th row: incr into stitch 1, k, incr into last st (eight stitches)

Repeat the fourth and fifth rows up to the eighteenth row.

Bind off

Dish Clothes

38. Gramma's Dishcloth

Tools and materials

Size 7 knitting needles

Cotton yarn (worsted weight)

Instructions

1st row: Knit

Knit 1, (k into the subsequent stitch at the front and back), knit 1

Knit 2, yarn over, knit until you finish the row

Repeat the last row until your needle has 45 sts remaining

Knit 2, yarn over, knit two together, knit until you complete the row

Repeat the last row two times more

Knit 1, slip the next 2 sts, yarn over, knit two together, knit until you complete the row

Repeat the last row until you are left with five stitches

Knit 2, knit two together, knit 1

Knit 1, knit two together, knit 1 so that you are left with three stitches

Cast off, then cut the yarn and sew in the ends.

39. Diamond Brocade

Tools and materials

Knitting needle

Cotton ice yarn

Instructions

CO 39 sts

1st to 6th rows: knit in the garter stitch

Knit 7, (purl 1, knit 7, repeat until you finish the row)

a) knit 3, purl 3, (knit 1, purl 1, knit 1, purl 5, repeat to the last nine stitches), knit 1, purl 1, knit 1, purl 3, knit 3

b) knit 5, (purl 1, knit 3, repeat to the last six stitches), purl 1, knit 5

c) knit 3, purl 1, (knit 1, purl 5, knit 1, purl 1, repeat to the last three stitches), knit 3

d) knit 3, (purl 1, knit 7, repeat to the last four stitches), purl 1, knit 3

e) knit 3, purl 1, (knit 1, purl 5, knit 1, purl 1, repeat to the last three stitches), knit 3

f) knit 5, (purl 1, knit 3, repeat to the last six stitches), purl 1, knit 5

g) knit 3, purl 3, (knit 1, purl 1, knit 1, purl 5, repeat to the last nine stitches), knit 1, purl 1, knit 1, purl 3, knit 3)

Repeat from (a) to (g) until you reach desired length.

Knit five rows using the garter stitch method, then cast off.

40. Crazy Eights Dishcloth

Tools and materials

Worsted weight cotton

Size 7 knitting needles

Instructions

CO sixteen inches

K one row

Shaping:

1st row: k to the last st, then turn

Even rows (from the second row to the 16th row): K

Odd rows (from the third row to the 17th row): K

18th row: K

Repeat from the first to 18th row seven times more.

Join from outside to inside of the mattress stitch, then knot up the inner circle. Sew in the ends.

Conclusion

Knitting is a really exciting hobby that has numerous possibilities. After you have mastered the basics, start with easy projects that take little time to complete and are less prone to mistakes. Some projects may tend to drag on, but don't worry. That simply means that you will learn more along the way.

To get yourself committed to the project, try to set a deadline for yourself: perhaps you want to gift the item to someone for an upcoming birthday or need to wear it on your next vacation. If you find your project going terribly wrong at the beginning, just remember that it is okay to be bad at something when starting out.! We might even go as far as to say that there is something truly liberating in sucking for one or two weeks before you finally get the hang of it!

All pros were beginners at some point anyway.

Printed in Great Britain
by Amazon